TALES OF THE

COUNTRY ECCENTRICS

FROM HERE
Come up and see me Sometime
FUEL
2L

TALES OF THE

COUNTRY ECCENTRICS

Tom Quinn

David & Charles

Photograph on page 2: Hulton-Getty Picture Collection

A DAVID & CHARLES BOOK

Illustrations by Alex Webb-Peploe

First published in the UK in 1996

A catalogue record for this book is available from the British Library.

ISBN 0 7153 0347 3

Printed in England by Butler & Tanner Limited
for David & Charles
Brunel House Newton Abbot Devon

Contents

1%

Introduction

The British have most famously been described as a nation of shopkeepers. The comment was meant unkindly but, being an agreeable people with a sense of humour, we somehow took the insult and turned it into a compliment. But for all that, it might have been truer to have described the British as a nation of eccentrics; how many of us, after all, have an aunt, an uncle or a grandparent who is regularly described as a bit of a character, or as wonderfully dotty, and if we live in a country area we will know someone, somewhere – either the village clock repairer, the local nurse, farmer or retired colonel – who strikes all and sundry as decidedly and delightfully eccentric.

One of the problems with the word eccentric is that it suggests so many things to so many different people: what is eccentric to one person is scarcely out of the ordinary to another. For the purposes of this book I have concentrated on people who are either in themselves rather eccentric because of the way they speak or their mannerisms, or because some aspect of their lives would be accounted eccentric by most of us. Thus Michael Levey, my lawnmower racer, is eccentric only in so far as he is a lawnmower racer – although his enthusiasm for and knowledge of his wacky hobby is none the less quirky for that. Likewise Ernie James; he fits the bill only in that the life of an eel catcher who uses medieval fishing techniques at the age of ninety-three would be seen by most of us as rather out of the ordinary. Merlin Maddock, by contrast, is the archetypal eccentric inventor, a wonderful man whose extraordinary brain has given birth to a thousand extraordinary creations of every conceivable type.

It has been said that the great days of the eccentric are long over; this is highly debatable and it is more likely, in fact, that we now have different kinds of eccentrics. Certainly most of us lead less isolated lives today and isolation was often a great cause of eccentricity; we are less superstitious, too, and fewer of us are engaged in curious or unusual occupations. The modern world in this sense has a lot to answer for, because it has reduced the differences between us as individuals and as communities; ubiquitous hamburger bars and identical housing estates have made our environment increasingly uniform and it is only the brave, the independent and the idiosyncratic – typified by those whose deeds are celebrated in this book – who add colour and interest to what would otherwise be a very drab world indeed.

At the more extreme end of eccentricity, modern medicine has enabled us to cure many ailments that led in former times to extremely bizarre behaviour. The hat maker of the past illustrates this perfectly. Hatters were almost invariably cited as particularly eccentric, which is why the phrase 'mad as a hatter' sprang up and became part of our language. We now know that it was the extensive use by hatters of mercury that led to their odd behaviour; absorbed into the body in even very small quantities, mercury affects people's behaviour markedly.

But eccentricities caused by mercury, or by lead used to thicken wine – another reason for the bizarre behaviour of many of our ancestors – are thankfully no more and the extremes of eccentricity have no place in this book, which is really a celebration of the kind of eccentricities which mark certain people out as individualists; as people whose occupations, hobbies, pastimes or general way of life make them entertaining and remarkable. I have therefore included the man who races lawnmowers in his spare time; the woman who has devoted her life to the sport of hare coursing; the man who keeps a golden eagle in his garden within ten miles of central London; the farmer who organises sheep races; and the world conker champion. If you met these people on the train you would hardly think them exceptional, but get to know them as you will in this book and you will realise that the British eccentric is alive and well.

It is the British interest in mad wacky hobbies, their love of the old ways, their refusal to compromise, their refusal to give up one way of doing something even when a more efficient way has been found, that makes us a nation of interesting characters unembarrassed by our refusal to conform. Many other countries can, of course, also boast plenty of eccentrics, America especially, but in America eccentricity can seem something of an affectation, the result of a desire to be noticed. In Britain by contrast people carry on their quiet, sometimes remote lives and they do as they please regardless of the judgements of the more conventional. This is the key to all the most delightful eccentrics.

A major part of this book also brings together portraits of great eccentrics of the past; their behaviour may seem more outlandish, more eccentric if you like, than that of their modern counterparts, but time and the telling and re-telling of the stories of their lives has certainly added to the legends that have grown up around them; and since the dead are unable to contradict the development of stories about them we must simply accept the legends as they have grown up. But that is all part of the magic of eccentricity; myths and legends grow about those who stick out from the herd, and in the case of these portraits from the past I think it is reasonable to describe them again and bring them back to life for a new audience. For eccentricity has a history, and the eccentrics of the past are first cousin to the eccentrics of the present.

Tales of the Country Eccentrics therefore collects together a number of eccentrics, past and present, who have lived over the last three hundred years, many long forgotten but still quite fascinating. It does not attempt to analyse the reasons for eccentricity, nor to define too closely the precise nature of eccentricity. It simply brings together a range of people loosely defined as eccentric but filling out the picture of Britain as a nation of fascinating non-conformists; a nation of people individual in their character and occupation and unquenchable in their enthusiasm for hobbies, sports and pastimes that the rest of the world may find utterly mad.

Hobbies and Hobby Horses

Few people take their private interests and enthusiasms terribly seriously, but when life and work become utterly intertwined, and pastimes all-consuming, there is no time left for the more mundane concerns of ordinary mortals, and the eccentric is born! Here is a rich selection of splendid individuals, from the inventor who makes wooden bicycles, and coats that light up when you laugh, to the man who spent his life collecting animals of increasing size and who became so captivated by them that he ate them rather than part with them when they died!

THE INVENTOR

Merlin Maddock

Pontycymmer, Mid-Glamorgan

Merlin Maddock is the archetypal eccentric. He is an inventor with more than two hundred patented inventions to his credit, ranging from highly complex designs for separating oil from water to extraordinary ideas for flying machines, carbon-fibre Welsh harps, jackets that light up when you laugh and wooden bicycles.

But that's only to start with because Merlin, who lives high up in the Gawr Valley in South Wales, also likes to challenge himself to make anything and everything from the most unlikely materials – such as his wooden padlock, his pond made from an aircraft jet engine and his jet-propelled scooter. He also has a car he built himself complete with a large aluminium key in the back which turns as you drive along. Now aged sixty-five, Merlin has spent his life coming up with wonderful ideas; a man of enormous talent, he has a remarkably fertile brain and although many of his designs are bizarre to say the least, he has also designed highly sophisticated, award-winning pieces of equipment. He was born in the village of Pontycymmer and though his former deputy-headmaster – at the time of writing in his mid-nineties – remembers him as a bright child, there was no real sign then of his extraordinary talent for inventions. What was clear, however, was that Merlin had the makings of a craftsman, and this is why, on leaving school, he decided to train as a locomotive engineer. Indeed, he was one of the last men in Britain to train on steam engines:

'I went to Stafford in the early 1950s,' he recalls, 'where steam trains were still being made at Bagnalls, and I was very lucky really because I caught the end of steam and the beginning of diesel. But those steam engineers taught me a thing or two, I can tell you, and it was a hard, disciplined apprenticeship that lasted six long years. But I liked the discipline and I admired the enormous skills of the older men, skills that have now vanished or remain only in one or two individuals like me who were lucky enough to have that training. Even the managing director at Bagnalls had started on the shop floor, and if he saw you doing something and you weren't doing it right he'd take his coat off and show you how to do it.'

After his apprenticeship Merlin worked in the mining division of the English Electric Company where he rose to become production engineer. He also travelled widely. However, the pull of his home village was always strong and in 1976 he returned to Pontycymmer and decided to turn what had been a hobby, harp making, into a business. But this was to be no ordinary enterprise because with harps, as with most things,

Merlin was determined to see if the designs could be improved. As he is the first to admit, he wanted to make harps better than anyone else.

'We made the first electronic harp,' he says proudly, 'and we made the first seventy-five-string triple harp that had been made in Wales since 1633 – mind you, it was a harp only ever played in Wales anyway. There was a problem with all the old harps because at the turn of the century they changed the pitch at which harps were played and the huge extra weight of the strings broke most of the old bone-glue harps. My triple harps were made from carbon fibre which could take the load.'

Once onto his favourite subject Merlin is quite unstoppable, but he clearly knows what he is talking about: his instruments have been used by some of the greatest harp players in the world. But when he sets his mind to a problem it is enthusiasm and dogged determination that carries him through. Take his furniture: most people buy theirs new or second-hand, but Merlin made virtually every stick of furniture in his house himself, from the dining-room table that has small clip-on satellite tables to the chairs with their spring-loaded seats and the extraordinary lamp standard which is made like, of all things, a chicken bone.

'You think I'm joking,' says Merlin with a funny twinkle in his eye. 'Well, I'm not. What you have to remember is that the chicken bone is actually just a very flexible spring, and it's a very good design which is why I chose it for that lamp. I'm going to make a chair on the same principle because the springiness will make it far more comfortable than a conventional chair.' Elsewhere around the house there are Heath Robinson-type shelves on chains that can be lowered or raised: 'I don't like bending over or stretching up,' says Merlin, 'so I've tried to make things that minimise inconvenience.'

In the kitchen all the cupboards are designed to reduce effort to the minimum, and Merlin has also invented what he calls an upside-down device for emptying the last dregs out of sauce bottles. The light above the dining table can be raised or lowered by repositioning a heavy bottle on the other end of a rope; and many of the lights in the house are operated by a foot switch – 'they're far more convenient than wall switches,' says Merlin. And there is a carving of a ship in a frame with sails that move according to the position of a barometer.

'You'll notice, too, that all the furniture has three legs,' says Merlin, 'because that way every piece has no choice but to stand flat!'

Merlin lives with his wife, Seena, in what was once the bakery in Pontycymmer; he virtually rebuilt it, and with its massive workshop it now provides an ideal base for a master inventor. One of Merlin's most prized creations is a completely wooden penny farthing bicycle. It doesn't take long to imagine the difficulties of making such a thing entirely from wood: the massive main wheel had to be delicate enough to be light, but also substantial enough to carry Merlin's weight. So how on earth did he do it?

'Well, you know, the bicycle was invented about a hundred years ago when a chap called Stanley invented the safety bike, but that was based on designs by Leonardo da Vinci. I wanted a boneshaker, a design that came long before the safety bike, so I calculated my weight in relation to the diameter of the wheel and the corresponding length of the pedals to create a bike that would be ideal for me in this very hilly area. My wheels work very well for me on these hills.'

And indeed, high up on his bright red boneshaker penny farthing Merlin is a familiar sight bowling through and around the village. The main difficulty with the penny farthing appears to be getting on and off: 'Once you're on you're fine for the rest of the day as long as you don't try to get off. That's when you have to really start concentrating again.' But Merlin has clearly mastered it entirely, for he has ridden thousands of miles in all weathers and over all kinds of terrain – he even rode blindfolded over the Severn Bridge once.

'I made the bike using the skills I learned as a locomotive engineer,' he explains. 'The wooden wheel is laminated for strength, and the whole thing took me four years to make. At first I used to practise round the village in the middle of the night because it did take some getting used to and I didn't want people to see me making an idiot of myself every time I fell off. I'm all right now just so long as I don't lose my nerve. But in those early days I knew that if I couldn't ride it properly I would be classed as the village idiot and I didn't want that. Basically the trick is to start it off, run behind it for a bit, and then climb up the back of it; but you're a long way up on that great wheel before you reach the saddle! Then there's the difficulty of getting off, which is the same procedure in reverse – only you might be going at a fair old speed, of course!' As well as practising at night, Merlin used to ride about in his workshop; but he is now a familiar and much-loved figure who travels great distances when he's in the mood.

'It's a very tricky thing to ride – looks easy, but it isn't at all,' he says with studied emphasis. 'Particularly when you're blindfolded, like I was on the Severn Bridge! You have to listen for when your guides shout to go left or right, and if you go too fast you can't control the steering, too slow and you fall off. I've done over a thousand miles for charity on that bike. I tried to ride to London to see Margaret Thatcher once. I got as far as Bristol and then got knocked off by a photographer, so I put my bike on the train and cycled from Paddington to Downing Street. And when I

made those wooden wheels it was the first time in over a hundred years that wooden wheels had been made in Wales.'

As well as designing furniture and inventing scientific equipment and new bits of technology, Merlin has written a children's book and a book which explains how Britain can be tidied up. 'Yes, I'm very proud of that, but no one would take it up,' he says ruefully. 'I can't find a publisher. It's a book about a character in the shape of a dustbin. I'll publish it myself one of these days.'

Merlin also spent a number of years designing and making toys. 'There's a lot of skill in that,' he says, 'because we made one basic design which could be modified endlessly to produce toy cars, toy lorries, toy aeroplanes. They went very well.'

As a craftsman, however, Merlin's main claim to fame was, and is, his harp making. When business was booming in the 1980s he had a sign outside the shop pointing to the sky which said 'Harp Factory turn first left'. So why did he give it up?

'After many years I found I had become terribly allergic to the timber we used – well, one of the timbers. It was so bad I just couldn't carry on. But when I started there were only three or four Welsh harp makers in Wales and now there are about twenty-five, and I'm sure the resurgence in the popularity of harps and harp playing was partly created by my own instruments which became very well known. We used to sell them for about £200 and now they change hands for nearly £2,000. I was particularly proud that I built that triple harp I mentioned; its design was unique because it was based on information I got from ancient songs and poems.'

The harps were made by a staff of thirteen based in the extraordinary clutter of Merlin's massive workshop; here, piled high in every conceivable space, are prototype inventions, drawings, plans, stores of timber and plastics, boxes, tins, oil drums, racks of chemicals and oils, files and boxes of documents, all stacked up in the most amazing profusion and apparent chaos. 'One of my best buys about twenty years ago was a great load of English oak,' says Merlin. 'It's very difficult to get, now.' Much of this timber has been used to make his household furniture.

His more remarkable creations include a wrist sundial, which looks plausible although he admits it doesn't actually work, and an artificial bandaged arm which he carries around and then leaves hanging over doorways and round the back of armchairs. He has also invented a mobile phone in the form of a special suitcase with an aerial and an ordinary circular dial and handset: 'When you're on the train you can pretend you've just had a call, and it's far more impressive than those ridiculous small yuppie mobiles.' The case is inscribed Prince Maddock in Welsh, in which language Merlin is fluent. 'It was my mother tongue until I was sixteen,' he says, 'and it's been very useful, really, since I've made a couple of Welsh language television programmes about my harp making.'

Merlin is also something of a collector: for example, he has a unique and massive collection of very early gramophone records, together with an antique wind-up gramophone to play them on; all the records are pre-1918 with a recording on one side only.

POLAROID

Although so many of Merlin's creations are wonderfully zany, there are one or two that can only be described as world-beaters – which explains why, in 1991, he won the Nat West BP Award for technology: this was for his invention of a device that could be used in the event of major oil spillage on the sea. Understandably cagey about exactly how this works, Merlin just says that it separates oil and water rapidly and with astonishing efficiency. 'I can't tell you what the secret is because it's a complete little thing with floats and a series of valves, and of course I don't want anyone else to know too much because I'm working on the prototype of an advanced model.'

For Merlin, nothing in life is ever taken for granted, which is probably why he conceived the idea of hanging his Christmas tree upside-down from the ceiling with an open umbrella underneath. 'Upside-down works very well,' he says with a grin, 'because the baubles hang away from the foliage, not into it, and presents can be stacked on top away from eager little hands. 'It also has the advantage that the moisture doesn't drain away, and every morning you simply pick up the umbrella, take it outside and shake it and all the fallen needles are gone. No more needles all over your carpet!'

Merlin also likes the odd practical joke. In Pontycymmer there is a tradition that details of funerals are pasted to lampposts. Merlin announced his own funeral once – it was a fund-raising idea, and in smaller print underneath the main announcement of his death there was an explanation. 'But people didn't read that far,' says Merlin, 'and they really thought I was dead! However, you can call "wolf" once too often in this village; when I got married I sent out the invitations on 1 April and no one came, they thought it was a joke.'

Among Merlin's more recent inventions is a waistcoat that generates heat every time the wearer laughs, chuckles or sneezes. 'I called my waistcoat the "Edwina", after Edwina Currie for a bit of a laugh, but it has quite a serious purpose really. She used to tell old age pensioners to stay warm by knitting so I thought I'd go one better. One day you could see a bus full of laughing pensioners going to the seaside for the price of a chuckle,' he jokes.

If some of Merlin's inventions are decidedly eccentric, so too are some of the ways in which he works. 'Well, when I've really got my mind on the job I sometimes don't go to bed for two or three days and nights at all. I just stay up and stay at it. It's much easier to work that way.'

Most of his inventions start in the kitchen sink, but he is always quick to patent

them: 'I've just invented something that may put a stop to burglaries, and all I have to do is pay £25 to register the idea; then eighteen months later it is published as mine. However, you have to have agents throughout the world for an invention because very few people can afford to patent something in every country – that would cost thousands.'

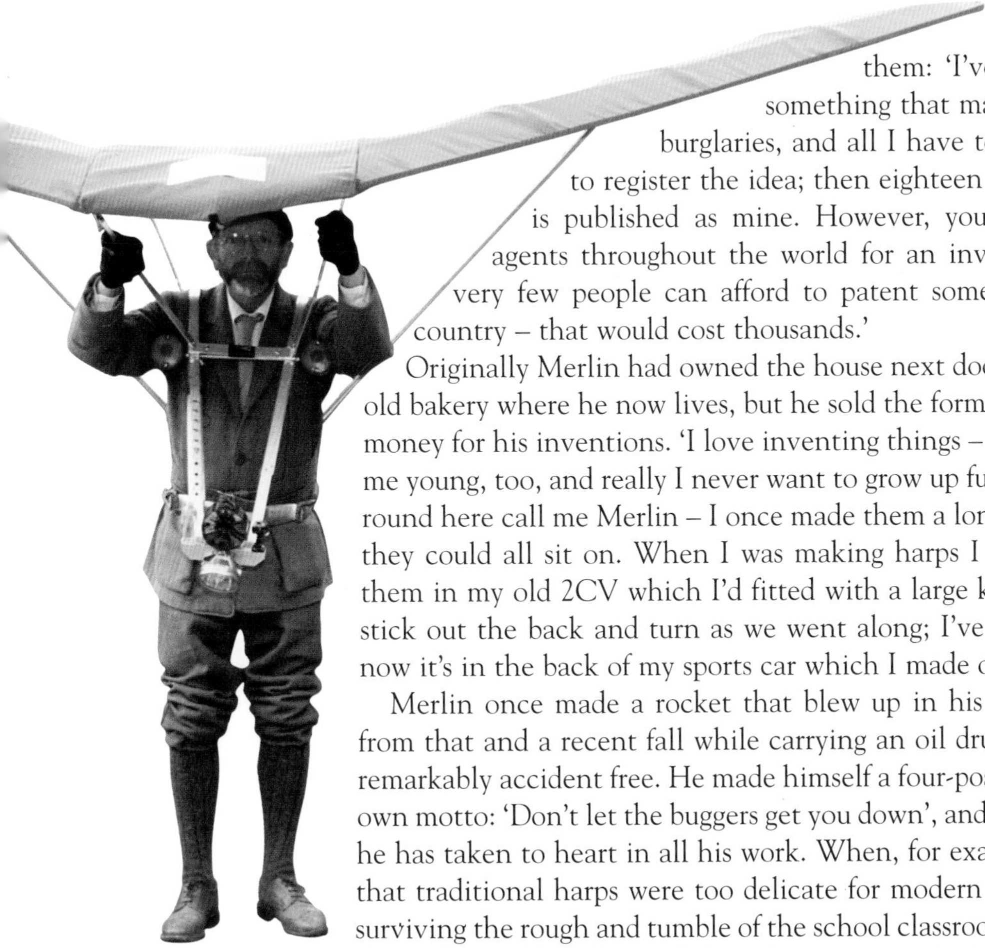

Originally Merlin had owned the house next door as well as the old bakery where he now lives, but he sold the former to raise more money for his inventions. 'I love inventing things – I think it keeps me young, too, and really I never want to grow up fully. All the kids round here call me Merlin – I once made them a long wooden train they could all sit on. When I was making harps I used to deliver them in my old 2CV which I'd fitted with a large key that used to stick out the back and turn as we went along; I've still got it, but now it's in the back of my sports car which I made out of a kit.'

Merlin once made a rocket that blew up in his face, but apart from that and a recent fall while carrying an oil drum he has been remarkably accident free. He made himself a four-poster bed with its own motto: 'Don't let the buggers get you down', and this is a maxim he has taken to heart in all his work. When, for example, he found that traditional harps were too delicate for modern work – such as surviving the rough and tumble of the school classroom – he thought about the problem for a while and came up with the idea of a carbon-fibre harp. He built the first of its kind in the world and took it to the Pan Celtic Festival in Ireland. To prove just how strong it was he proceeded to drop it from a great height onto a concrete floor. It was unscathed by the experience, so he threw it out of the car window on the way home and it was still undamaged. His flying machine has yet to take off, but his propeller-driven scooter was a hit when he rode it through the streets of London.

Merlin's travels as a serious scientist have taken him all over the world, but most recently to Amsterdam. Besides his luggage he took with him a jar filled with jelly into which he had inserted several plastic mice, painted brown and with their tails cut off; the idea was that at some stage he would be able to say that the whole thing was 'Hamster jam'. When he arrived in the city he was spotted wearing an enormous plaster over one ear, in memory of Van Gogh.

PANAM
BURGER

CONKER CHAMPION

Charlie Bray

Cole Henley, Hampshire

Charlie Bray is one of those old-fashioned countrymen with a perfect cottage garden, a great love of trees, plants and animals and a wild enthusiasm for a sport that came to an end for most of us when we left school. For Charlie is a world champion – at conkers. And when he isn't harvesting conkers, organising conker demonstrations or playing in the championships, he studies the conker, tries out different preservatives on it, stores it up in great quantities from good harvests and discards it from poor years. His fame as Mr Conker has spread so wide that he is regularly asked to plant conker trees!

A small, neat, highly energetic man in his mid-seventies, Charlie is also a devotee of topiary – ornamental hedge clipping – and has won a number of national prizes for his beautiful yew trees, clipped into spirals, pyramids and giant chess pieces. A gamekeeper by profession, he lives in a lovely brick-and-flint cottage on an estate at Cole Henley, a village just outside Whitchurch in Hampshire. 'The great thing about being here is that I'm surrounded by conker trees,' he says with a smile. When visitors meet him – and he is always welcoming in spite of the fact that a lot of people are keen to meet him – he is usually surrounded by what he describes as his conker tackle: suitcases full of conkers, jars of preserved conkers and his championship conker gear: old cricket flannels and a cricket jersey cov-

ered with conkers. He also has a bow tie made from conkers, and he has conkers all over his playing shoes and playing hat.

Twice world champion, Charlie has been involved in top class conker matches since 1978. He was world champion in 1979 and again in 1986 – 'I've still got my winning conkers from 1986,' he says proudly and he has long been a steward of an event which now attracts competitors from all over the world.

The world championships started in the early 1960s when a group of fishermen, disappointed by their lack of success on the River Nene in Northamptonshire one Sunday in October, retired to the Chequered Skipper pub in Ashton. To while away the time they picked up a few conkers from the trees that grew nearby and organised a competition, the loser to pay for the beer. That's how it all started, although Charlie, one of the leading lights of the event today, explains that the competition is far more professional now than it was in those early days.

'These days there is a committee which spends the whole year organising each competition. It's always held on the second Sunday of October to commemorate that very first competition, and it's always on that green outside the Chequered Skipper.' There are also events for women, and a children's championship has been introduced. But for Charlie, all the fun is in the build-up to the event and in the atmosphere.

'Oh, we get about four thousand people on the big day now,' he says. 'And apart from anything else we raise a lot of money for charity; to date it's something like £107,000!'

Originally the championships were highly exclusive, and new competitors were only accepted as existing members dropped out. But soon the pressure to take part was so great that the numbers crept up to the current figure of around 128 (and including women and children it would make a total of about 300). With such an increase in numbers came the need for carefully set-out rules, as Charlie explains:

'Well, it's not that it's become a deadly serious competition, it's just that without rules a single game of conkers can go on for ever, with people delicately tapping each other's conkers and hoping theirs won't break first. That's why we have a five-minute rule: if someone hasn't won after five minutes we have a tie-breaker, which gives each competitor nine strikes in sets of three. If a conker still hasn't broken, the man or woman with the most hits – and remember, it's very easy to miss! – is the winner. And you do get a lot of people donking, which is what we call it when you just tap the thing.' Charlie on the other hand, as he is quick to demonstrate, is positively murderous when he builds up his conker swing:

'I go for the side swing, because you get the conker to travel a lot further that way, although it can be dangerous if you don't know what you're doing because then it is much more likely that you will tangle your conker string with that of your opponent. Do that three times and you are disqualified.' And if Charlie sounds like an authority on the subject of conkers, that's because he is; he gives demonstrations at fairs and fêtes all over the country, as well as at schools and charity events. He was even invited to America to play conkers, and has played on the *Big Breakfast Show* : 'I seem to remember that I managed to hit the presenter with my conker,' he recalls with a smile.

When he went to America, Richard Branson provided the transport in the form of a Jumbo jet specially decorated with conkers. The importance of world championship conkers was also reflected in the fact that accompanying Charlie was a film and sound crew

WORLD
CONKER
CHAMPIONSHIPS
ASHTON 1986

amounting to fifteen people. But despite his growing fame, Charlie remains endearingly modest about the whole thing:

'It's all a laugh, really, wherever you are playing. The first man I played in America was the customs officer. Then I tried to play someone as he came jogging past me in the New York marathon, and finally I played with an American policeman. They also wanted me to play with television people, on top of the Empire State Building – anywhere they could. In four days and dozens of games I only lost once!

Charlie is understandably reluctant to give trade secrets away, and apart from preserving conkers in various fluids – treated conkers are not allowed in the world championships – he is only prepared to divulge one or two little tricks: 'Well, you can nurse your conker; in other words, you don't hit as hard as you might if yours is starting to look weak, because if you go easy your opponent may smash his in trying to smash yours.'

Training is another big part of the successful conker player's life, so much so that Charlie has built a conker practice stand out of an old BBC microphone: 'It helps people sort out their swing, and because they are hitting a conker-sized rubber ball they're not constantly breaking their conkers.'

Charlie has even played a game with a squirrel for the cameras, although 'the little devil went and bit my best conker!' he confesses. But the big question is: what makes a top class conker? 'Well, ideally you want as close to round as you can get. Because if you think about it, a flat-topped conker, however big and powerful it looks, is going to offer your opponent's conker a good hitting surface. A nice round conker means that your opponent's blows will glance off, doing less damage. But at the world championships none of this makes any difference because you draw your conker, already drilled and on a leather lace, from a special bag and if you win the first round with it, it is withdrawn from the competition. A fresh conker is drawn for the next round. That's why there's a lot of luck in it. In the second or any other round you could by bad luck pick a conker that is not as good as the one used in the previous round. That means you start with a serious disadvantage.'

Privately, however, Charlie experiments with all sorts of preservatives to see if he can produce the ultimate conker: 'I've tried various types of wood preservative and the old schoolboy trick, vinegar, but the best so far is linseed oil which makes them hard and stops them drying out. It's the kernel you have to protect; that's the bit you have to toughen up.'

Charlie is a great believer in dressing the part when he is competing or demonstrating, which explains why he has conkers sewn all over his playing gear; with his conspicuous dress and his television appearances, he has become something of a media star. Back at the world championships, however, it was decided that, like other sports, it was time conkers introduced drug testing. The pronouncement on one player was that he had failed the test...because he didn't have enough alcohol in him!

But if you think Charlie is a bit obsessed by conkers you need to meet another stalwart of the sport; Charlie knows him well: 'Oh yes, Vic Owen. He's a very interesting character. He's known as King Conker because every year, as well as opening the proceedings by ringing his bell and declaring the championships under-way, he always adds another long string of conkers to the huge wreath of conkers he already carries: one string for each year, making well over thirty now. The only trouble is that with that many conkers round his neck he can't stand up any more. Still, he's working on the problem!'

A NUN ON THE RUN

Marjorie Hotston Moore

Milborne Port, Somerset

Marjorie Hotston Moore is a self-confessed eccentric former nun with a passion for frogs, Lego and gadgets of every kind. She lives in a tiny, 300-year-old cottage called Moore's Mini Mansion at the top of a Somerset hill; with its three-feet-thick walls and tiny rooms, the cottage seems the perfect setting for a woman who is by any standards a bit of a character. Wonderfully dressed in lime-green trousers and with a floppy woollen hat wedged almost permanently on her head, Miss Hotston Moore darts about the house throwing logs on the fire and explaining her personal history and philosophy of life.

Marjorie at about three years old with Auntie Rose

'I'm terrible for saying the wrong thing, I know that, but there's no point in keeping quiet if you're not happy with what's going on. I do speak my own mind, but I think it only gets me into trouble with bureaucratic types. I may not be very popular in some quarters, particularly with those in authority, but I'm well liked by the people in the neighbouring cottages, though I know they think I'm a bit mad. And I have so many toys in the house that I'm also a real favourite with the local children – they're in and out of the house the whole time.'

Marjorie Hotston Moore started life sixty-five years ago in rural Norfolk, where she was born in a big house overlooking the sea near Sheringham. Her father, she says, was the eldest son of a long series of eldest sons stretching back to a king's illegitimate son; because of the royal connection the family was given a house and land. 'That splendid house was only sold in my grandmother's time,' she says proudly, although she cannot remember precisely where the house is. But the family name can be traced back to Henry VIII's reign at Aldingbourne Church register.

The house in which she was born was pretty substantial, too: 'It had twenty bedrooms, and my parents had intended to run it as a sort of small hotel or boarding house. But the war came, and as it was in what was described as an invasion area it was used by the army for billeting officers' wives; at one time we had twenty evacuee children from Dagenham, too. Most people didn't have much to eat in war time, but we did very well because we had a big garden with plenty of fruit and vegetables, and of course all the local keepers had gone to war so the poachers were having a field day; they would regularly turn up with pheasants, rabbits and hares.'

It was about this time that Marjorie conceived the idea of becoming a nun.

'When I left school I decided to become a nun at Westcliff-on-Sea, but my interest had very little to do with religion. I wanted to be a nun because I thought you only had to walk around all day looking holy, and I thought that would be rather nice. It seemed such a pleasant life, but they quickly decided I wasn't quite holy enough and kicked me out. I was a postulant for a year – that's the stage before you become a novice. I was sixteen, and I remember being told that they didn't think I had a vocation and to come back when I was twenty-five; but of course I never did. They still write to me even now, trying to save my soul! The main thing I didn't like about being a nun was that it was jolly hard work, and I think I was a little too unorthodox for them.'

Unorthodox certainly seems to be one way to describe the hilarious scrapes and escapades that she has spent her life getting into. Initially, however, one might be forgiven for wondering quite how a sixteen-year-old novice nun could be unorthodox while spending her days in a strictly ordered Anglican convent; but as Marjorie explains, it wasn't too difficult: 'I found the convent very dull occasionally, so I used to sneak out at night. I'd put a big old coat on, tuck my robes up on the way out and then, I'm ashamed to admit, I used to take sixpence from the poor box to pay for my roller skating. I loved roller skating but it wasn't allowed, which is why I had to sneak out every Saturday and get the bus to Canterbury. Often I'd get on the bus and the conductor would see I was a nun and not charge me. That was wonderful because it meant I could afford a knickerbocker glory as well as the skating!'

It was while she was at the convent that she began working with children; this was to become her life's work, although her earliest memories of working with children are typically full of fun and humour: 'We used to look after disabled children from London who'd come to Westcliff-on-Sea for their holidays. I remember taking a disabled child down to the sea in a sort of wicker carrier on wheels, normally used for what were called spinal cases. I was pushing it with one child in the basket and a couple of other children walking with me. I thought it would be much more fun if we all jumped in and raced down to the beach, so we did. We shot down the hill and ended up with a terrific crash in the sand at the bottom! The children thought it was great fun, of course. We used to get down to the beach frequently like that. So much more fun than just pushing it quietly down the hill – and woe betide anyone who got in our way!'

From those early days in Westcliff-on-Sea she has always worked with children and young people, and mostly in rural areas. However, her tutor at the convent had organised a place for her at Birmingham University, which is where she next arrived – although 'I rather fear I caused havoc there, too,' she says with a grin, but declines to elaborate. She trained as a social worker and worked in a National Children's Home in various parts of the country for several years.

Gales of laughter greet much of Miss Hotston Moore's decidedly individualistic style of narration, but her early life does seem to have been a rush of jobs and mad incidents all over the south of England: 'After leaving three National Children's Homes I also worked in Ipswich as a trainee nurse, but I only lasted a week – I couldn't bear the hospital atmosphere, and ever since then I've hated hospitals; they definitely make you ill. At the end of my week's nursing I decided I didn't want to leave in the normal way so I climbed out of a window in the middle of the night and went home on the milk train in case the sister caught me. I sent my brother on later for my trunk.'

'After trying different jobs I went home to my parents who had moved to the outskirts of Worthing. I went to the West Sussex College of Art where I learned about textiles, spinning and weaving, and dyeing. I also did painting and pottery, and learned how to make baskets of willow and cane. But while I was at the art school I met the supervisor from the local training centre for the handicapped, and it was through her that I began teaching handicapped children.'

Boundless energy and a capacity to try anything and everything new seem to be the hallmarks of Miss Hotston Moore's character; but running in tandem with her remarkable energy and determination there has always been a tendency to be accident prone: 'I have been rather unlucky, it is true. It was at about this time that I had a bad motoring accident and was in a coma for three months. When I woke up I discovered all my possessions had been sold – they hadn't thought I was going to recover, so the nurses had to buy me enough clothes to stand up in!

'All I remember about that time is that the hospital staff spent a lot of time trying to feed me custard and I didn't like the stuff. I used to blow it all over them, which soon put a stop to it! I also used to spit out all the sleeping pills they used to give me. I didn't sleep much then and I don't now, and I'm quite happy about it; I just don't need as much sleep as other people.'

Once out of hospital – 'they told me I'd never use my hands again, but I showed them' – she answered 'thousands' of job advertisements in *The Church Times*: 'I could get a copy for nothing by pinching it out of the church,' she says. Ever in search of new adventures she was then offered a job at a hostel for destitute women in London.

'I accepted that job because I needed one that brought with it somewhere to live; I wouldn't have taken it otherwise because I don't like city life – I've always thought of myself as a countrywoman. Anyway, there were forty-seven women and they were only allowed in at night; sometimes they were violent, but most were really very nice. I worked there seven days a week, twenty-four hours a day for four years. Most of the time I was the only member of staff so there was no way I could take time off. One of the women who was very friendly used to offer me money because I earned so little there – she was a prostitute earning about £17 a night while I earned £3 10s for a whole week!

'A friend bought me a bottle of expensive scent which I didn't ever use so I used it to spray the bowls of artificial flowers that were left on the tables. That gave the whole place a lovely country smell. After four years I went to another hostel, this time in Camden, where we looked after teenage girls. They were fine, but their boyfriends were dreadful; I remember one turned up once in a violent temper so all the girls and I sat on him and pulled his hair when he tried to move, until the police came.'

Even in a job that many would find soul-destroying, Miss Hotston Moore managed to find both humour and adventure. 'One of the funniest things about that place was the guard dog – it was matron's dog really, and she thought it was absolutely vital for our security, but whenever there was trouble it used to hide under a bed somewhere and refuse to come out until things had calmed down! I was there for a year, and then went to Reading where I worked with girls on probation.'

Worried about not having a settled domestic base, Miss Hotston Moore spotted the little cottage where she now lives during a holiday thirty years ago, and immediately snapped it up. She is well known and much loved locally, and she has become a byword for getting things done – 'I keep badgering them till they realise I am right – don't give up, that's my motto!' She loves the surrounding countryside, enjoys plenty of long walks and though long retired is as busy as ever.

'When I came to this house I knew I was going to be happy. I got a job with handicapped children and studied eventually at Southampton University. I taught in several local schools and then worked with violent teenage boys: I still get postcards from some of them, especially at Christmas, although we were not completely successful with all of them I'm afraid, so some of the postcards arrive with a prison postmark!

'I've done and still do all sorts of things. I used to take elderly people from the outlying villages to their day centres, for example, but they used to fight like hooligans in the back of the car so I had to give it up! I am a professional dog walker for several of my neighbours, and I make my own carpets and baskets still. I have ten looms, a spinning wheel, a pottery wheel, an electric bandsaw and a treddle fretsaw.'

Her greatest claim to fame, however, is her vast collection of Lego sets. She first became interested because she found Lego so useful with children, but as her knowledge of the subject grew, so too did her enthusiasm. 'I think I've got nearly £4,000 worth of Lego in the house, including some real collector's stuff. I'm a member of the Lego Club and I've got the T-shirt to prove it – I even went all the way to Denmark to visit

Legoland a few years ago. I also have four train sets. People laugh at the idea of Lego, but architects use it to build models of their buildings. I think I'm right in saying that I've got more Lego sets than any museum *and* you can make full-sized cars with engines out of it!'

She has come a long way since those days in Norfolk and Westcliff-on-Sea, although her early enthusiasm for the church has not stood the test of time, as she explains in characteristic fashion: 'I'm not really religious now, in spite of my year in the convent, and I hardly ever go to church – I find Christians rather off-putting.' Instead she spends her time indulging her various interests including a more recent passion for frogs.

'Yes, I spend a lot of time collecting frogs of every conceivable kind, ceramic, plastic, terracotta, china – I've got hundreds, although they tend to disappear on holiday to various children round the village. In fact frogs are all right, but now I'm in my sixties I thought I ought to try something a little more exciting, so every year I go on an adventure holiday and I've also taken up canoeing and abseiling. I've tried surfing, too, but I have a terrible tendency to fall over before I even get in the sea. And the wet suits are such a problem.

'One of my greatest disappointments was that I injured my back and had to give up my Yamaha motorbike. That really was a bit of a blow, I can tell you – whizzing along the country lanes on a big machine was one of life's sweetest pleasures.'

THE SHEEP RACER

Edward Dorrell

Telford, Shropshire

On a small farm in the heart of the Shropshire countryside you can enjoy a day at the races on any weekday from March to October, but it will be a day with a difference, for Edward and Carolyn Dorrell of Hoo Farm near Telford organise sheep races. Now in his forties, Edward is hugely enthusiastic about a sport he virtually invented. 'I believe there is another farm where they also have sheep races, but they don't jump fences. And we're very careful not to force our animals to race; if they show signs that they're not enjoying it, we retire them.'

Hoo Farm is one of those places that children love to visit: as the need to diversify became more pressing because of falling farm incomes, Edward and his wife Carolyn realised that, along with other attractions such as ice cream and ostriches, sheep racing would be great fun and might also help to bring in some extra income. 'It's still just a bit of fun, but we do allow a little harmless betting – the children pick a sheep and bet fifty pence on it. However, the important point is that it adds to the attractions of the farm which is really a combined working farm – we have four hundred ewes – and animal centre.'

Edward, a wonderfully ruddy-faced man with huge boots and much-repaired corduroy trousers, keeps pigs, sheep, cattle, deer, llamas and ostriches, but at the heart of the farm lies the one-furlong sheep steeplechase track; indeed it is Edward's proud boast that his is the world's only steeplechase track for sheep. 'The other farm only races on the flat, but we're in our fifth steeplechase season now,' he says, 'and it's just become more and more successful. We've even got serious bookmakers looking at what we do – one came down a couple of times, and I know it was well worth his while, though being a bookmaker he never actually said as much.'

As regards training the sheep to race, Edward attributes his success to a few simple rules: first, all the racing sheep – there is a stable of eighteen in all – are orphan lambs which had to be reared by hand; this means they are used to close human contact. Second, they are encouraged to race simply because they know there is plenty of good food at the end of the track. That track is precisely a furlong – 220 yards – and includes two turns and four fences, each about a foot high. Edward considers that his background as an amateur jockey helped him organise the races and design the fences, each of which is named.

'It's just like horse racing: first we put them under starter's orders, then the starter gets them going – but the sheep know I've already gone down the track with a good big bucket of feed, so when I shout to my wife to let them go they hear me at the other end of the field and know quite well what it's all about. And they're rarin' to go! Each race normally lasts about forty-five seconds, which works out at the sort of pace that would produce a six-minute mile.'

Edward is scornful of those who say that the whole thing is unnatural and that sheep shouldn't race; and anyone who has seen sheep galloping around a field will probably agree with him. As he explains: 'I'll give you an example of how keen they are. We've got a sheep called Black Midget, one of our best racers, and on this particular day we'd left him in the ostrich paddock because he wasn't racing. We sorted out the race that afternoon, got them going – and suddenly Black Midget appeared out of nowhere! In fact he'd cleared a four-foot high hurdle because he couldn't bear to be left out; *that's* how keen they are!' And animal welfare is firmly at the top of the Dorrells' list of priorities:

'We let visitors get close to all the animals,' explains Edward, 'but if anyone is ever seen annoying or upsetting an animal we ask them to leave. It's the same with the sheep. Even when they retire we don't simply send them to market; we put them in a retirement paddock because, having been hand-reared, we know them by name and they are like friends of the family.

'We always noticed how competitive sheep can be when we were feeding them out in the field – we would joke to each other about which one would be the first to get to us; and suddenly we thought well, why not organise the thing properly?'

Races normally consist of eight or nine runners, each wearing a hat and sporting a proper number cloth. Edward's father-in-law made the fences, known as Darner's Ditch, Spinner's Chair, Woolly Leap and Fleece's Brook. The racing sheep are all males, and ages range from a one-year-old novice to a veteran at five years; they each run once a day, except for one or two remarkably agile animals which would win every race if they were allowed to – these super-athletes are only allowed to compete once in every three or four days so as to give the others a chance. The racing sheep all have special names: Bib Bonz, Dumpy Dilon, Larry Lamb, Hairy Harry, Simple Simon, Charlie Farly and Lucky Leggy.

Like most sheep they are shorn in spring, although losing the weight of a heavy fleece doesn't seem to speed them up; says a genuinely baffled Edward, 'No, I'm not sure why, but it doesn't. In fact in some cases losing their fleece seems to slow them down.' Some of the sheep apparently dislike the going when it is firm, others find it helps; they are also definitely creatures of habit with a rather short attention span. Edward explains that if they see a cow or an ostrich unexpectedly looking over the rails on a bend they may all stop or even run the wrong way: 'It's just anything they haven't seen before. They are easily distracted. A photographer once left a tiny remote-control camera on a post, and even that made them stop!'

None of the sheep is pure bred – 'they're a real mix, we just call them Hoo sheep' – but they are undeniably part of the social round at the farm. 'We even have a Sheep Grand National,' says Edward proudly, 'and an Ascot evening, where people watch a few races and then dine and dance in the house.'

The Hoo Sheep Races are now so famous that visitors come from all over Britain and America to watch them, although one suspects that part of the attraction is Edward's breathless race commentary over an impressive Tannoy system. His speed of delivery would put many a horse-racing commentator to shame, and in their hats and number-cloths the sheep somehow manage to look like really serious competitors – which, of course, they are. Races are always held at three o'clock and after the main event there is a training race for those sheep that did not compete in the main event.

'A chap who does our shearing and has worked with sheep all his life came to watch a race and I remember his eyes were out on stalks,' says Edward. 'He just kept repeating that he'd never seen anything like it and that he just couldn't believe it; but as I said to him, it's all in the training.'

For Edward and Carolyn, eccentric ideas are a way of life: they also run a pick-your-own Christmas tree scheme, where people simply come along, select a shovel – Edward makes sure he has plenty – select a tree and then start digging. Apparently they love it.

COBWEBS AND CASH

Daniel Dancer

Daniel Dancer was born in 1716 at Harrow Weald in Middlesex where his father owned a considerable amount of property and land. Little is recorded of his earliest years, but by his early twenties he was sharing the family house with his sister. On the rare occasions she ventured out she was usually dressed in layers of rags – 'a mixture of male and female attire tied round with a ravelling of hemp' – and would be armed with a broomstick or pitchfork to attack anyone who ventured onto her brother's property.

Their house was patched and boarded and repaired to an extraordinary degree, and hardly a stick of their furniture remained in one piece because Dancer used wood from it to carry out repairs. Not only did he have to keep out the weather, he also had to plug every hole to keep out the hordes of neighbouring cats attracted by the huge numbers of vermin that roamed the house.Thrift was carried to absurd lengths. For example, a neighbour called one day and found him pulling the nails out of a pair of bellows: he needed the nails, he said, to fix a piece of leather over a hole in the wall and he thought the bellows could spare the nails and save him the expense of buying any. 'Undertakers, trunk-makers and bellows-makers are the most extravagant fellows in the world in their profusion of nails,' he said.

Each Saturday Dancer would buy a 3lb piece of beef of the cheapest kind and boil it with a dozen or so hard dumplings; that would then have to sustain both him and his sister until the following Saturday. Occasionally their diet would be supplemented by bones that Dancer came across during his long walks – yet for all this he had an annual income of £3,000, at a time when a labourer was expected to be able to keep a family of six on £30 a year.

Dancer was taking his usual walk across Harrow Weald Common one summer morning looking for bones, sticks, rags and anything else that might be useful to eat or to repair the house, when he came across a dead sheep. The sheep had clearly been dead for some time, but for Dancer this was a rare prize and he dragged it home in triumph. He and his sister lived on that sheep for weeks: they boiled it, roasted it and made it into pies, but when they were down to the last few dozen pies Dancer locked them away in a chest because he felt they were being eaten too quickly.

When his sister lay dying Dancer refused to call a doctor because he did not want, as he put it, 'Wickedly and wantonly to oppose the will of God. If the girl has come to her latter end, nothing can save her.' Miss Dancer had planned to leave her fortune to a neighbour, Lady Tempest, but she died before making a will and for the next few years Dancer and his two brothers fought over the legacy. Finally they went to court, and it was decided that Daniel should have over half his sister's money after he had argued that that was the cost of her board and lodging for thirty years!

Back at his house Dancer continued just as before: he washed every three weeks in the horse pond, and in spite of endless patching his clothes revealed more than they

concealed; in cold weather he twisted ropes of hay up and around his legs. He bought one shirt a year, never washed it and kept it until it fell apart, and he never had his house swept or cleaned in any way. Yet when the house was burgled the robbers could find absolutely nothing.

In spite of half-starving himself continually Dancer was hugely sentimental about animals, and his dog was always fed on the best meat and milk. He kept a horse, too, but only had its front two feet shod, to save money. He walked to London once to invest £2,000 and while waiting outside an office in the city he was mistaken for a beggar and given a penny. He was delighted, and told the story to anyone who would listen for the rest of his life.

Lady Tempest, his neighbour, eventually persuaded him to buy a hat to protect himself against the weather, though it was only a second-hand one. He wore it for some time, and then Lady Tempest noticed that he was out in all weathers hatless again. When she asked him what had happened he told her with great pleasure that he'd sold the hat for sixpence more than he'd paid for it.

Though he ate almost nothing, he loved trout steamed in claret, but he would only eat it when Lady Tempest had it cooked for him and sent over. In the course of one winter such a dish of trout once arrived, but it was cold. Dancer wouldn't light a fire to warm the dish and he knew that if he ate it cold it would give him bad toothache, so he put it between two pewter plates and sat on it until it was warm enough to eat.

During his last few years it was said that he slept in a sack with a hay beehive on his head. He never had his own snuff although he would accept it gladly when it was offered by others. However, he never actually took it: he merely put each pinch in his own box and then when it was full he sold it! His favourite occupation night and day, but mostly at night when he couldn't be seen by anyone else, was to visit the hundred and one holes and corners about the house and barns where he had hidden gold, notes and silver coins.

When he died in 1794 at the age of seventy-eight, his heirs found £2,500 hidden in a dungheap. In an old jacket nailed to the stable door they found £500 in gold and notes, and there were banknotes in every cushion and bolster, in the sofa, in milk jugs and bowls. In more than twenty holes in the chimney £200 was found in soot-blackened notes. In an old cracked teapot there was £600 in notes and on a small slip of paper left lying on top of the notes was a scrap of paper on which Dancer had written: 'Not to be too hastily overlooked.'

THE CAMPAIGNER AGAINST SITTING

Stanley Green

Stanley Green died at the age of seventy-eight in 1992, having spent nearly thirty years parading Oxford Street in London with a placard warning against the dangers of protein. He sold thousands of hand-printed leaflets (at 12p each) explaining why lustful feelings were induced by 'fish, birds, meat, cheese, egg, peas, beans, nuts and *sitting*'. He had worked for many years in the Civil Service before starting his one-man campaign against lust in the mid-1960s. Although the campaign was centred on London, Stanley was actually a countryman, having been born in rural Hertfordshire.

'Protein makes passion,' he would say to anyone who would listen. 'If we eat less of it, the world will be a happier place.'

He produced his leaflets on a small press in his tiny flat in North West London; the tenants below often complained about the terrific sounds of thumping and crashing on print day. Until he qualified for a free bus pass he would cycle each day to Oxford Street in his raincoat, cap and wire-rimmed spectacles, and always recalled with pleasure that motorists reading the board on the back of his bicycle would toot their horns and wave. 'I've known coaches pass,' he said, 'and everyone has stood up and cheered me.'

He was occasionally spat at, but he was rarely upset by abuse, explaining that people only attacked him because they thought he was a religious person. He would often concentrate his efforts on cinema queues, using such opening gambits as 'You cannot deceive your groom that you are a virgin on your wedding night'.

A LEGAL GIANT

Judge James Crespi

Christened Caesar James, Judge Crespi was born in 1928 and educated at Cambridge. He was a remarkable eccentric by any standards, although by profession he became a quite brilliant advocate. He claimed that he saved his most eloquent speeches for the Fleet Street wine bar El Vinos, where apparently the wine waiter always greeted him with a clenched fist across his breast and the words 'Ave, Mr Crespi'. He also became enormously fat, though luckily all the taxi drivers knew him by sight so he never walked anywhere – his bulk made it virtually impossible – except one novice cabby who once mistook Crespi's wing collar for the dress of a waiter, and dropped him at the staff entrance to the Savoy.

He married a woman he met in a night club, but for reasons he was never able to recall. The marriage was described by Crespi as 'Obviously a case of mistaken identity' and it lasted less than a week. When asked if he regretted anything in life he simply said 'Being mistaken for Lord Goodman, whoever he is'.

A REMARKABLE SEMI

William and Walter Straw

Walter (left) and William Straw

When William Straw's mother died in 1937 he decided that he would keep the family house as a shrine to her memory and to that of his father who had died in 1932. In fact until William died in 1990, he and his brother Walter, who died in 1975, never touched a thing in the house, down to the newspapers left on tables, hats on pegs in the hall and tins of food in the kitchen.

When officials entered the house after William's death they discovered a small, perfectly ordinary semi that had lain untouched and undisturbed for more than five decades, a perfect, probably unique survival of a house whose very ordinariness made it extraordinary. William Straw (born in 1898) had lived in the house with his brother Walter (born 1899) since the 1930s when their parents had died. They lived according to a strict routine, never married and had no close friends in the town in which they'd spent their lives. They had no social life to speak of, and callers and visitors were never invited into the house.

But the story really begins with the brothers' parents, Florence and William Straw Sn, a grocer and seed merchant. Their business having prospered, the Straws moved into the house in 1923 and immediately spent £100 – a huge sum at the time – having it totally re-decorated and fully furnished. Because Worksop was then distant from centres of fashion such as London, the décor and furnishings are actually just as they would have been in a house of this kind at about the turn of the century. The house itself was built in 1905.

After the death of Florence in 1937 William, who had been teaching history at London University, returned immediately to Worksop and set up house with his brother Walter who had run the shop after their father's death. While Walter cycled to work each day until the shop closed in the 1970s, William stayed at home and did the housework. From that time on the two men effectively cut themselves off from the rest of the world.

No one knows whether it was simply the shock of their parents' death that turned the brothers away from the changing world, but it appears that the house became something of a shrine. Nothing their parents had owned or bought was ever moved or thrown away – even the calendar on the sitting-room wall is dated 1932 – but towards the end of their lives the brothers clearly became aware of the value of what they had done, for they began carefully to label various items of furniture and pictures explaining their provenance.

Visitors to the house, which is now owned by the National Trust, quickly realise that this is an extraordinary time-capsule. Step through the front door into the hall and you see William Snr's homburgs and trilbies hanging on the pegs where they were left half a century ago; his pipes and tobacco are still above the fireplace; in the kitchen, fifty-year old jars of Bovril stand in the cupboards; in the sitting-room piles of newspapers from the 1930s have been left as they were in William Sn's time. All the furniture is solidly Edwardian, heavy, dark and usually mahogany, the woodwork of stairs and door-frames painted and grained dark brown; sombre wallpaper covers the walls of every room. In the kitchen there is an enamelled range, a butler's sink and glossy green painted walls and linoleum.

Walter and William with their parents around 1925

Receipts and Christmas cards from the 1920s and 1930s were found carefully preserved in boxes, and in the chests of drawers in the bedrooms Florence's clothes were still neatly folded and packed away where they had been placed when she died. In other drawers were found beautifully preserved examples of Florence's own mother's clothes dating back to the middle decades of the nineteenth century.

Even the light bulbs at No 5 date from the 1930s – and when the house was first opened up in 1991 they still worked! Each room is filled with the sort of clutter the Edwardians loved: heavily framed sepia photographs and sombre pictures hang from picture rails; on the mantelpiece below the overmantel mirror in the sitting-room are photographs, an elaborate clock, numerous tins and boxes of letters and documents. In the bedrooms the 1930s bedclothes, carefully protected by the brothers with newspaper, still lie on the beds.

The brothers' own daily lives reflected their total rejection of the modern world. They grew their own vegetables, mended their own clothes and never threw anything away. They washed their clothes on Mondays and baked bread on Saturdays. Neighbours never came to the house. They were never rude to people, just remarkably self-sufficient, but they didn't like women. Neighbours remembered that on rare occasions when cousins visited, their wives had to sit outside in the car.

The brothers lit coal fires every day to keep the house warm – there was no other heating – and on Sundays, dressed in their dark suits and bowler hats, they walked quietly together to church. They never owned a radio, television, car or telephone.

But if they were eccentric they were also highly intelligent, William especially so. Widely read, he was deeply interested in his own family history and in that of the town in which he'd spent his life.

THE GAMBLING MISER

John Elwes

John Elwes was born in about 1730 into a family of notorious misers; they had lived in Southwark for generations, and made their money from brewing. His mother is said to have died from malnutrition in spite of having tens of thousands of pounds in the bank, and although John was apparently an exceptionally bright child, he rarely opened a book after leaving school; in fact as the desire to make money grew he gave up everything else, including riding which had been a passion in his youth.

In his twenties he began to visit his uncle, Sir Harvey Elwes, but he always changed into rags before he reached the house, so terrified was he that his uncle, a famous miser, would be offended at his decent clothes and disinherit him. Later, when he himself was bitten by the miser's bug, he refused to educate his own sons because he thought it would give them grand ideas about spending money rather than keeping it.

The two men, uncle and nephew, would sit by a fire made with one stick and completely in the dark, sharing a glass of wine until bedtime; they would then creep upstairs, still in the dark, to save the cost of a candle.

When he came into his inheritance John became fanatically stingy. He would walk from one end of London to the other in the heaviest rain rather than part with sixpence for a coach; he ate maggot-infested meat; he would never light a fire to dry his clothes; he wore a wig that had been thrown into a ditch by a beggar, and a coat that had gone green with age – it had belonged to a long-dead ancestor and had been found blocking a hole in the wall of the house. When he rode to London – he was an MP for more than ten years – he would always carry an egg or two in his pocket and sleep in a hedge rather than pay the cost of lodgings, and he always rode his horse on the grass verge instead of on the road for fear that his horse's shoes would wear out too quickly. He owned houses all over London as well as an estate in Suffolk, but took a few pieces of furniture with him each time he travelled about rather than furnish each house.

Yet in spite of this parsimony he rarely collected a gambling debt if it was owed to him by someone he liked, and he was himself a very keen gambler, parting with thousands at a go when the mood took him. He could also be enormously generous and considerate; for example he once rode sixty miles to help two elderly spinsters threatened by an ecclesiastical court. He died in 1789 at the age of fifty-nine, and left more than three-quarters of a million pounds to his two sons.

A HOUSEFUL OF ANIMALS

William and Frank Buckland

William Buckland (1784–1856) was Dean of Westminster and first professor of geology at Oxford. He was also a fanatical naturalist. To prove the efficacy of bird droppings as fertiliser he once used great quantities of it to write the word 'guano' on the lawn at his Oxford college. When the summer came and the grass had grown well the letters could be clearly seen. At his house you were almost certain to be offered roast hedgehog or a slice of grilled crocodile steak – and if you partook, the chances are that one or both came from an animal that had roamed Buckland's house and garden a little earlier as a pet!

Travelling to London on his horse one dark wintry night William got lost, but trusting to his extraordinary sense of taste he simply dismounted, picked up a handful of earth, tasted it, shouted 'Uxbridge!' and went on his way.

William's friend Edward Harcourt, Archbishop of York, was, like Buckland himself, a great collector of curiosities and had managed to obtain what was believed to be the shrunken, mummified heart of Louis XIV. He kept it in a snuff box and rashly showed it to William. 'I have eaten many things,' William is reported to have said, 'but never the heart of a king.' He then popped it into his mouth and swallowed it whole.

Frank Buckland (1826–80), William's son, was if anything even more eccentric than his father. He was a naturalist and collector of animals of every description; he also helped found the Society for the Acclimatisation of Animals in the United Kingdom which introduced all sorts of exotic animals into Britain in an attempt, it was said, to widen the roast beef diet of the British. At the society's annual dinner likely items on the menu would be dormice on toast followed by boiled sea slug, roast kangaroo and grilled parrot; at its first dinner in 1862 the meal included tripang, 'Much like a horse's hoof'. Throughout his life Frank dined regularly on rhinoceros, elephant and giraffe: he had friends at the zoological gardens who would contact him when an animal died. He was once given a whole batch of giraffes that had died in an accident.

At Winchester, Buckland was famous for wandering round with his pockets full

of live snakes, frogs and mice, and he was often found wading into a deep lake to retrieve a specimen he had left in the water to rot so that he could more easily remove the flesh from the skeleton. He kept a live owl, a buzzard, a magpie and a racoon in his room, and the descendants of a white rat that escaped from his pocket can still be seen amongst the local population of Winchester school rats. He also kept a monkey, a chameleon and numerous snakes.

Away from the classroom he spent much of his spare time cooking mice and eating them out in the fields; when a master discovered what he was up to he didn't ban it, but simply told Buckland he would have to cook his mice *in* the school. Buckland visited Winchester hospital regularly and would swop eels and trout for various pieces of the anatomy of patients who had died. He was once heard to mutter while gazing admiringly at a fellow pupil's head: 'What wouldn't I give for that fellow's skull!' Unlike most pupils who used their pocket money to buy sweets and chocolate, Buckland would pay his fellow pupils 6d each if they would then let him bleed them.

By the time he got to Oxford, where he narrowly missed a scholarship, he had a small menagerie in a specially constructed zoo outside his rooms; here he kept snakes, a monkey, a chameleon, an eagle, a jackal and a bear which he named Tiglath-Pileser after an Assyrian king, Tig for short. The eagle once escaped and was discovered perched in the college chapel. Buckland rarely expressed an interest in any subject other than natural history, and said of politics that when he couldn't understand a parliamentary bill he always translated it into Latin in which language it apparently made more sense.

When entertaining fellow undergraduates his normal dress was a bright blue coat and a big red hat with tassels. Dressed like this he loved to leap up every few seconds and blow loudly through an enormous wooden horn.

When he left Oxford Buckland decided to become a surgeon, but first, like most young men of his background at the time, he left for an extended period of study abroad. With his scientific interests Germany must have seemed a natural choice for Buckland whose eccentric habits did not meet with universal approval. During one journey he was threatened with eviction from a coach after it was discovered that he had twelve live tree frogs hidden in his pockets; their deafening croaking, of which Buckland was oblivious, infuriated the other passengers who were kept awake for hours. He also tried to bring home a large quantity of big red slugs, but while he was asleep they escaped and he woke to find that one of them was making its way precariously across the bald head of the sleeping passenger opposite. Rather than face a scene Buckland left the slugs where they were and leapt off the coach.

Back in England at a big garden party Buckland turned up with his bear, Tig, in tow. He had dressed it in a scholar's cap and gown and proceeded to introduce it to the assembled *glitterati*, including Florence Nightingale, several princes and Napoleon I's nephew (their reaction is not recorded!). Tig eventually ended up in London Zoo after being caught trying to rob a sweet shop.

Buckland always said that the best part of his foreign travels was the time he spent in Paris where the laws that governed the obtaining of bodies for dissection were far more lax than in England. He was particularly pleased because French bodies tended to be fresh!

At work at St George's Hospital in London, Buckland had become a member of the Royal College of Surgeons in 1851, but he resigned a year later for reasons never fully explained. His time at the hospital did, however, produce a number of amusing incidents. He dined out for many years, for example, on the tale of the poor woman with a bad cough who had come to him regularly every week and each time asked for larger and larger quantities of a certain cough mixture. Eventually he became suspicious and, following her, discovered that she had been making the mixture into tarts and selling them outside the hospital.

Buckland was nineteen when his father was made Dean of Westminster; while he was living with him in the abbey precincts his eagle escaped again and was found sitting on one of Hawksmoor's magnificent towers. The bird was captured by Buckland using a live chicken on a very long pole.

Once when travelling with his monkey, Jacko, in a bag Buckland was about to buy a railway ticket; just as he was handing his money over, Jacko popped his head out of the bag at which the stationmaster insisted that the monkey would have to be paid for, too. After a long fruitless argument, an extremely exasperated Buckland pulled his pet tortoise out of a pocket and asked what fare he would have to pay for that. 'No charge for them, Sir, them be insects,' came the stationmaster's reply. This same monkey accompanied Buckland everywhere during his time in the Life Guards. He dressed it as a troop corporal major, but when he discovered that it had been ripping the buttons off his coat he had it demoted to private and dressed it accordingly.

In spite of the fact that his house was already filled with animals, both stuffed and living, Buckland continued to haunt the dock areas of London in search of specimens; although he was adding continually to his collection, he never threw anything away.

In 1850 he married Hannah Papps, a coachman's daughter. Luckily for Buckland she seemed to enjoy his mania for collecting animals as much as he did – at least there is no evidence that she objected to the hordes of monkeys one observer once saw sitting round the Buckland fire: 'They did terrible damage and bit everyone, but he loved them dearly,' he commented. But rats could also be seen running everywhere, over desks and tables and around the mongoose and donkey that also had the run of the place. Having so many animals frequently led to minor disasters – for example when two antagonistic animals met on the stairs and began a terrible fight. Also, Mrs Buckland had reared a South African Red River hog boar from infancy. It was an enormous beast, and at dinner one evening it crept into the dining-room and wedged itself under a guest's chair; then, alarmed by a sudden noise, it got up and ran out of the room but with the guest still in his chair on the pig's back!

Visitors frequently bumped into extraordinary animals in the most unlikely places: one woman tripped over a hippo at a turn on the staircase. The hippo was destined for the pot, but the woman had been frightened out of her wits – though Buckland merely told her that a hippo was a rare and valuable animal. 'They don't grow on trees you know,' he is reported to have said. When his animals grew old or died Buckland often ate them anyway, but he abhorred cruelty. He had eaten many things in his time, but pronounced mole 'poo' and bluebottle 'worse'.

A keen historian, he once went through nearly 3,000 coffins in the vaults of St Martin-

in-the-Fields looking for the body of John Hunter, the eighteenth-century surgeon whom he admired enormously. Almost the last coffin contained the right man who was re-buried with great ceremony and given a proper memorial.

Buckland was appointed Her Majesty's Inspector of Fisheries, and in this capacity was responsible for making sure that migratory fish were able to get up Britain's rivers. While helping construct a salmon ladder on one river he put up a sign for the benefit of any salmon stuck in the weir below the as yet unbuilt ladder:

'No road at present over the weir,' it read. 'Go downstream, take the first turning to the right and you will find good travelling water upstream and no jumping required.'

His appointment as fisheries inspector had a lot to do with his wide-ranging knowledge of natural history, and a major part of his work involved travelling the country in search of spawning salmon and trout. So enthusiastic was he that he claimed he had hatched some 30,000 salmon in his own kitchen sink during his career. And if he had odd things in the sink you could always be sure that he would have even more extraordinary creatures, including humans, in the house. Dwarves, giants, rat- and bird-catchers were all invited, for Buckland delighted in everything that added to his sense of human diversity. A giant Irishman who visited him wrote his name on the ceiling of the drawing-room; when a spring-cleaning session led to its being obliterated, Buckland was furious.

On one occasion he was sent to Ireland to inspect a salmon fishery, and decided he wanted to know what it was like to be a salmon; so he undressed and lowered himself into the fastest part of the salmon race. 'How on earth do they do it,' he was heard to mumble. It was at about this time that he began to grow oysters, and opened a fish museum at St Martin's Court in Leicester Square. He also took over the editorship of a journal called *Land and Water*. Energetic and highly artistic, he next began to make magnificently accurate plaster casts of fish. He once bought a huge fresh sunfish at Billingsgate, threw it down into his kitchen and made a plaster cast of it. He then found that the cast, which of course was rigid, was so big he couldn't get it out of the kitchen again.

Often he had so many specimens in various stages of decomposition that the whole house stank unendurably, but he never seemed to notice, probably because he was intrigued by the processes of decay. In 1866 he wrote: 'I do not think rats will eat putrid meat...I have lately discovered in my cellar the body of an eagle which I had forgotten and which was rather high. I know there are rats in my cellar because I will not allow them to be killed as I consider they do me good service in eating the bits thrown away in the dustbin. But these rats had not touched the eagle...'

For Buckland, however, it was sometimes difficult to avoid eating his specimens even when he really didn't want to, and good-looking ones were always in particular danger. 'Directly I am out of the way,' he wrote, 'if they look good to eat they are cooked; if they stink they are buried. What am I to do? I have to keep a sharp lookout in my house...' Nevertheless, towards the end of his life his interest in the culinary quality of all sorts of animals intensified. He tried a porpoise's head but thought it tasted like lampwick, and in *Land and Water* he once offered readers otter steaks; all they had to do was write to him and he would send a steak by return.

Buckland had his own remedies for a number of ailments; for example, he never wore a coat because it caused colds and 'flu, and if he couldn't sleep he sat up all night eating raw onions. But away from what may now seem his greatest eccentricities, Buckland actually did a great deal to improve our treatment of animals: he campaigned for many years for humane methods of slaughter in abattoirs, and he disliked intensely the indiscriminate slaughter of animals for sport. Moreover he was said to have had infinite patience with animals and humans, and he was certainly unfailingly generous; he often rescued down-and-outs and former friends who had become ill or had fallen on hard times. He believed, too, that inanimate things had feelings, and planned to write a book on the spitefulness of objects: if a lamp didn't burn properly he said it was sulky; and he punished his luggage once by thrashing it.

But some of his vaguely scientific ideas are still difficult to swallow. He suggested fattening fish, for example, by hanging a horse's leg or half a sheep from a branch overhanging the water. Maggots would breed on the rotting flesh and fall continually into the water where they would be eaten by the fish.

Understandably, he is most remembered for being eccentric: children used to gather outside his London house to see the extraordinary collection of freaks who went continually in and out, and on one occasion Buckland arrived home to find all his servants standing in the street because two badgers had got out of their box and were running amok in the house. Another time a guest spotted one of Buckland's boots apparently moving independently around the sitting-room – a mongoose had got inside it and was running around trying to get out.

At night Buckland often went cockroach hunting – he would dash into the kitchen in his nightshirt holding aloft a syringe filled with benzine and then try to inject any fleeing insect he could catch up with.

A visitor was once horrified to come across Buckland in the kitchen dissecting a large, far-from-fresh animal, and in between cuts he was helping himself to huge spoonfuls from a giant cauldron of stew.

He hated boots and usually went around barefoot; once, on a train, his boots so irritated him that he kicked them off and they flew out of the window. Nothing daunted he walked to his hotel in his socks. Five feet 'and a half' tall, and almost as broad, he was described variously by his contemporaries as 'sentimental, gushing, wild and sensational, and impetuous'. He never took care of his own health, always travelling hatless and coatless however cold the weather. He died at the age of fifty-four, and wrote in his will 'God is so good, so very good to the little fishes that I do not believe he would let their inspector suffer shipwreck.'

John Buckland, Frank's great-great nephew, lives today in Hawick, Northumberland; he shoots and fishes, and continues the family tradition of delightful whimsicality.

JUST MAD ABOUT SNUFF

Margaret Thomson

When she made her will in the early part of the nineteenth century Mrs Margaret Thomson stipulated that her coffin be filled with all the snuff handkerchiefs that were unwashed at the time of her death; she also wanted to be surrounded with snuff in her coffin. Six of the greatest snuff takers in the parish were requested to be her pall-bearers, and each was asked to wear a snuff-coloured hat. Six girls were instructed to walk behind the hearse each with a box of snuff which they were to take copiously for their refreshment as they went along.

The priest who officiated at the ceremony was invited to take as much snuff as he desired during the service, and Mrs Thomson left him five guineas on condition that he partook of snuff during and throughout the funeral proceedings. In return for a bequest of snuff, her servants were instructed to walk in front of the funeral procession throwing snuff on the ground and on the crowd of onlookers. And throughout the long day of the funeral, snuff was to be distributed to all comers from the door of the deceased's house.

ANIMAL COLLECTOR

Walter Rothschild

Decidedly but brilliantly eccentric, Walter Rothschild (1868–1937) hated speaking to people, was blackmailed out of a fortune by his mistress and trained three zebras to pull his carriage along the Strand. Unfitted for the normal routes into public life that Rothschild elder sons tended to take, he began a natural history museum that eventually grew into the biggest private museum in the world.

He would pay almost anything for a rare or unusual specimen, and by 1920 after working in virtual seclusion for years for eighteen hours a day he had amassed some 2,000 complete mounted animals; 200 heads, 300 antlers, 3,000 stuffed birds, 700 reptiles, 1,000 fish, 300,000 bird skins and 200,000 birds' eggs. He was a brilliant if utterly obsessive zoological classifier – a sub-species of giraffe is named after him.

Once while being driven through Hyde Park he spotted a chauffeur standing outside a stationary car with a folded rug over his arm. Rothschild immediately shouted at his driver to stop. He leapt from the car, explaining that the rug in the other chauffeur's arms was made from the pelts of tree kangaroos. Having waited till the owner of the rug arrived he refused to leave until the rug had been sold to him.

Financial troubles eventually meant that Walter had to sell part of his magnificent collection. He was so upset by this that he quickly fell ill and was dead within a few months.

THE PUDDING KING

Ernest Onians

When Ernest Onians, a reclusive antiques collector from Suffolk, died aged ninety in 1985, executors found that they could hardly get into his big Georgian watermill because it was packed from floor to ceiling with valuable antiques. Despite their value the antiques – pictures, clocks and furniture – were simply piled and stacked everywhere in huge confusion all over the house.

More than one thousand paintings including numerous old masters were found propped against the walls and there were almost sixty clocks, dozens of violins, manuscripts, sculpture, furniture, and thousands of smaller items. Onians' passion for collecting had so overwhelmed him that he'd even filled all the outhouses and sheds with valuable objects.

Onians had made a fortune through his business – he produced Tottenham Puddings – and though he spent millions of pounds on antiques, in over forty years of marriage he never bought his wife a present.

He always dressed in the scruffiest clothes and such was the chaos in the house that burglars who got in once took only small amounts of cash; everything else looked like junk! As the house filled with furniture and pictures his servants and staff gradually had to leave – there was simply no room for them – as his nephew John Onians recalled: 'The cleaning lady was dismissed for vacuuming a valuable carpet too briskly, and he once said he wanted to take his whole collection to the grave or leave it to his dogs!'

Aristocrats and Academics

Buried in books and drowning in money – too many brains and pots of cash have always produced wonderful eccentrics! Men who turned sensible words into hilarious nonsense, or who swallowed vast quantities of dangerous chemicals in the pursuit of science; those who locked themselves away and built huge underground palaces, or who became so reclusive that they refused to speak to anyone – except by letter.

LANDOWNER AND PIGEON FANCIER

Lord Niedpath

Stanway, Gloucestershire

James, Lord Niedpath, comes from a family that would be considered remarkable by any standards, for the Niedpaths, also earls of Wemyss (pronounced 'Weems'), have lived in the same mellow Tudor sandstone house in Gloucestershire since 1530. Indeed the estate of Stanway, tucked away in a particularly leafy corner of the county, has changed hands only once in 1,260 years, which takes us neatly back to the early eighth century. The present Lord Niedpath, however, a distinctly young-looking forty-eight, has kept his extraordinary house just as his ancestors left it. Little has been changed in three hundred years and the various rooms, their walls hung with a full complement of family portraits, have none of that newly bought look so characteristic of the more recently ennobled.

Like his house, Lord Niedpath has a wonderfully lived-in look; wearing a pinstriped jacket that looks positively shot to pieces he sits in his library surrounded by a remarkable clutter of old film canisters, letters, invitations, notebooks, dusty ledgers, envelopes, cameras and documents of every conceivable kind. Surrounding this clutter are superb pictures, a magnificent Strawberry Hill Gothic fireplace, and glorious eighteenth-century bookcases packed with beautifully bound antiquarian books.

Stanway was built by unknown hands on the typical medieval E-plan; its staircases, each tread made from a great solid triangle of native oak, seem somehow to meander rather than take the unwary anywhere direct, and if you don't know your way, it is quite easy to find yourself lost or to discover that, having imagined you were at one end of the house, you have actually ended up at the other. But for Lord Niedpath, who has written a short and highly entertaining history of Stanway, the house is as familiar as his own face: 'We don't know who built it,' he says, with a dramatic sweep of his arm, 'but we know a lot about how it came to be owned by the family.' And it is this fascinating story that Lord Niedpath explains in his own inimitable way to the many hundreds of visitors who come to the house each year.

A modest, entirely unassuming man, he is also an unusually informal host. Anyone may ring the house and make an appointment to look round individually or in a group. Charges are kept very low, and as often as not Lord Niedpath conducts the tours himself, much to the delight and astonishment of his visitors, particularly Americans. Extremely knowledgeable about his family and its history, he works tirelessly on the upkeep and restoration of the house and grounds; but visitors to this particular historic house won't find areas roped off or signs saying 'Do not touch', as you might expect: you are more likely to be invited to sit on an historic sofa, although you would do well to check first that Lord Niedpath's dog hasn't left a large bone on it! But how did the family come to Stanway in the first place?

'In 715 Stanway was given by two local Mercian magnates, Odo and Dodo, to the abbey of Tewkesbury,' says Lord Niedpath, with a practised air. 'Four monks were established here, but they held the land in what was known as *frankelmoin* – that is, in return for their prayers for the souls of the founders of the abbey and their descendants. In 1530 Sir William Tracy of nearby Toddington declared in his will that he relied on faith, and not the prayers of the monks for his salvation. For his pains his body was dug up and burnt by the church which, perhaps understandably, caused widespread revulsion. William's younger son, Richard, used his influence in 1533 to obtain from the abbot at Tewkesbury a lease on Stanway. On the expiry of Richard's male issue in 1677 Stanway passed to the Toddington branch of the Tracys, and the last of these Tracys, Susan, married Francis Charteris, Lord Elcho, son of the seventh Earl of Wemyss in 1771. The house has remained in the ownership of the earls of Wemyss since then.'

Though he has told the story countless times, Lord Niedpath – who will become the thirteenth Earl Wemyss when his father dies – manages to make it sound fresh each time; but then, he is something more than an amateur historian.

After Eton he studied at Oxford both as an undergraduate and as a postgraduate; his doctoral thesis, published in 1981, was entitled *The Fall of Singapore and the Decline of the Eastern Empire*. After Oxford he trained as a land agent, and then took over at Stanway where his grandmother had lived previously. Lord Niedpath had spent his own earliest years in Scotland, but having taken over at Stanway he threw himself into the business of running the estate's 4,999 acres.

With his tousled brown hair now streaked with grey and wearing his elegantly crumpled shirts and battered jackets, Lord Niedpath – followed virtually everywhere by his dog – is a consummate performer when it comes to guiding visitors round the house. And in every tour he clearly relishes the point where he shows his visitors his collection of eighteenth-century hair: apparently it was the custom for visitors to Stanway to leave a piece of their hair behind in an envelope as a memento of their stay. But if that is an ancient practice that has died out, there are several others at Stanway that are carried on to this day, one in particular being the business of collecting the tenants' rents in what is known as the Audit Room, using a special revolving table with a drawer for each tenant's rent book; this table was made in 1778.

The rent-collecting ceremony is one of the last of its kind in the country, requiring as it does the tenants of the various cottages and farms actually to come to the house and hand over their money in person. Each payment of rent is placed in a special well in the centre of the table, which is fitted with secret compartments for notes, with a secret catch to prevent unauthorised removals of money. Rent audits of this kind were apparently almost universal before 1914, but Stanway is one of the last estates still to adhere to the practice.

If the rent table is an extraordinary survival, so too is the shuffleboard in the great hall. One of the oldest in the world, it is 16ft long and made from one solid heart of oak; it even has its original brass counters, and is at least 250 years old. The game is played much as shove ha'penny, though on a large scale.

Lord Niedpath's delightfully idiosyncratic appearance and manner are matched by a curious yet endearing passion for pigeons. Having raced them as a boy he decided he loved having them around so much that he brought several baskets of birds from the family home in Scotland and installed them in the attic above his bedroom at Stanway.

'I thought it was a bit much when British Rail tried to charge me a child's fare for each pigeon!' he says with a gesture of outrage.

'But when I lie in bed now I can always hear them, and it is something I greatly enjoy.'

Up in the dark, cobweb-filled attic there are two small wooden chairs permanently positioned near the little roof enclosure where the birds live, and individual visitors are taken up here to sit and watch the birds. Lord Niedpath sits in one chair (having dusted it first) while the visitor or friend sits in the other (also carefully dusted by Lord Niedpath) in order better to contemplate a dozen or so apparently very ordinary pigeons. All around is the dust of many centuries, but none of this bothers Lord Niedpath who takes great pains over his birds, feeding them carefully himself every day and providing them with bathing water from his own rooftop tank. 'They have bred here,' he says with evident relish. 'And I hope that when eventually I create an opening in the roof so that they can fly in and out as they please, they will think of this as home. I don't like the idea of keeping them shut in up here for so long, but they do have to become completely acclimatised to this place; if I let them out too soon they will just fly off and won't come back.'

Out in the grounds Lord Niedpath strides about hatless and in a thin jacket in the pouring rain. With his dog in attendance and stopping only to dig for a while in a recently excavated drain, he explains the attractions and some of the difficulties of living at Stanway: 'Well, as you can see, it is an extraordinarily beautiful house – although I live here I never get bored by it – but because it is listed grade 1 it is a nightmare to get anything changed or repaired. We receive a bit of help from English Heritage and similar organisations, but for example it cost £300,000 just to replace the roof on part of the house, so you can imagine the annual repair and maintenance bill. That's why we're open every Tuesday and Thursday and by appointment at other times. The money raised goes straight into running and repair costs.'

Undaunted by the difficulties of bills and regulations, Lord Niedpath is planning extensive restoration work in and around the house. The grounds once boasted a canal and a cascade – a painting hanging in the great hall to this day shows just how spectacular they were – and Lord Niedpath hopes to reinstate both. He also plans to open up two great windows long since blocked up: 'I will if I can get permission,' he says with a piercing look. 'It can be so awkward with the house being listed, but it would transform the drawing-room.'

But what of those pigeons in the loft?

'Oh, they are marvellously clever creatures. I could watch them all day – they are very intelligent. That's why I don't really like fantails or doves, because they have no brains. A friend had a pigeon that always knew when she was on her way home – that's how intelligent they are, and I love the wonderful noise they make. It's very soothing, and it is actually a more complex sound than people think. Like their mating dance – intricate and complex.'

Back down the narrow ladder from the attic into the house and Lord Niedpath strides ahead, arms waving as he points out the major features of some of the great rooms, such as the Chippendale exercise chair with its long thick springs. Lord Niedpath's ancestors apparently took their exercise by bouncing vigorously up and down on it. Elsewhere dotted about the house are numerous photographs of Lord Niedpath in tweeds, breeches and stockings, as well as other family portraits, and a doggy family tree. A tradition started by Lord Niedpath's father decrees that family labradors, whatever their individual names, are always given the prefix 'Smelly'.

THE HUMAN GUINEA PIG

J. B. S. Haldane

Born in 1892 into a fiercely academic family, John Burdon Sanderson Haldane spent much of his childhood lying in the meadows around Oxford with corn stuffed up the legs of his trousers hoping that the local pigeons would land and risk their lives by foraging around his thighs. But this was just the beginning of a life devoted to science, Oxford and eccentricity.

Haldane's father, John Scott – known to his friends as Uffa – was a notorious eccentric, but he was also a man far ahead of his time in many respects. Few other scientists objected at the time, but John Scott hated experiments on animals, which was why he insisted on conducting dangerous or potentially painful experiments on himself. He once hired a ship, filled its hold with rats and then tested the effectiveness of suphur dioxide as a rat poison by pumping the sealed ship full of it. He ran back and forth between the dockside and the boat, insisting that his son do likewise, holding his breath and seeing how many dead rats he could remove at a time without passing out amid the noxious vapours.

Young JBS often accompanied his father on his more bizarre journeys of scientific discovery. Together they once crawled miles along a narrow seam in a coal mine looking for a pocket of methane gas. When they found it, Uffa made the young JBS stand up and recite a whole speech from Shakespeare. JBS did as he was bid and promptly fainted, which was precisely what his father had intended. When he had recovered he was told, 'You have just learned that gas, being lighter than air, always rises.'

In 1904 JBS was sent away to Eton where he was once beaten every day for a whole week; but he was already showing signs of the brilliance at science and mathematics that was to lead to his distinguished career. At New College, Oxford his glittering progress continued unabated, although he did manage to find time to continue studying a subject that had fascinated him as a child: his sister Naomi's collection of more than three hundred guinea pigs. For her part Naomi only ever taught them tricks.

In 1914, along with many of his student colleagues, Haldane left New College and enlisted. In the trenches he distinguished himself by an astonishing lack of concern for his own safety and a total refusal to wash. Earl Haig is reputed to have said of him: 'he is the bravest and dirtiest soldier in my army!' Injured by the blast from a massive shell he awoke to find himself being driven toward a field hospital by the future King Edward VIII. Many thought that Haldane's experiences in the trenches had left him relatively unscathed, but he always said that nothing after the war seemed real. He once wrote that he believed that his life after 1918 had all been entirely imaginary. 'Perhaps I will eventually wake up,' he mused.

Back at New College he resumed his academic studies and his teaching, but became increasingly interested in politics. A lifelong socialist, he was employed as a bouncer during Labour meetings in Oxford during the 1920s and he once pulled a heckler out of the hall by his nose; not such a feat when you consider that, by this time, Haldane weighed something approaching seventeen stone.

Throughout the years of his fellowship at New College he made himself ill by consuming large quantities of dangerous chemicals as part of experiments that he refused to carry out on animals. On one occasion he ate so much hydrochloric acid that he rode home on his bicycle feeling, as he said himself, like a demented devil. On another occasion he was discovered running furiously up and down a long staircase to test the effects of almost two ounces of bicarbonate of soda that he'd swallowed.

Blithely unaware of the fact that other people did not always take kindly to the idea of being experimented on, he once caused a stampede at a scientific symposium in Scotland by making pepper gas to demonstrate the kind of thing soldiers had to put up with in the trenches. People ran from the hall clutching their throats, their eyes streaming. The lecture was abandoned.

At about this time he began writing for newspapers and magazines, and it was these articles that really brought him to public attention; but although he made a good part of his living from journalism he despised all journalists and newspapers. 'The only thing you can believe in a newspaper is the date,' he used to say.

After many years at Oxford he suddenly decided to move to Cambridge

where his lectures became ever more unpredictable, and he would often get in a hopeless muddle with slides and notes. However, for all that, he was also unfailingly kind to his students. One young man came to him worried that, having been arrested for his bad driving, he might be found guilty in court and this would blight the rest of his career. Haldane was sympathetic but non-commital; but unbeknown to the student he spent days tracking down the chief prosecution witness, a notorious drunk, whom on

the morning of the trial he so plied with whisky that his evidence was discredited and the student escaped with a warning. The student later expressed his profuse thanks in Haldane's rooms whereupon he was presented with a huge drinks bill. 'The man was a serious drinker,' said Haldane, 'and I was forced to consume rather more than I was used to on a weekday morning.'

A few years after arriving at Cambridge he decided to get married, but there was a slight hitch because his bride-to-be was already married. However, this was no problem for Haldane. First he went to see the vice-chancellor of the university and announced that he was about to commit adultery. Knowing that for the divorce to go through the other side would need proof, Haldane enlisted the help of the private detective who had already been hired by the other side! He told him precisely which hotel the adulterous act would be committed in and even gave him the room number. Haldane was caught, just as he'd planned, the story appeared in the newspapers and his girlfriend got her divorce. But as a result of all the publicity surrounding the case he lost his readership at Cambridge – and he was furious.

In Cambridge, as in Oxford, he cycled to work every day, in an open-necked shirt winter and summer; his bicycle was about fifty years out of date. In summer he enjoyed swimming in a local pond, but always naked, and as he swam serenely up and down he smoked his pipe continually.

At home and now married, he spent months training his cat to sit on top of the door into the sitting room and to attack anyone who came in. He was devoted to all animals, even the spiders which eventually infested the house. He always refused to have even their webs removed. He loved to quote the Rousseau disciple who, when asked by a lawyer friend to crush a spider, replied: 'If some superior being should say to a companion, "Kill that lawyer," how should you like it? And a lawyer is more noxious to most people than a spider.' Still smarting over his treatment by the authorities at Cambridge following his adultery, Haldane left Cambridge in 1932 and went to London.

In 1945 he divorced his first wife and married his research assistant. By this time his temper had become notorious in academic circles; it had worsened considerably, probably as a result of the large quantities of chemicals he continually consumed for his experiments. Once when the BBC asked if they could film a discussion between Haldane and three other eminent scientists, they secretly agreed to film the men separately because they thought Haldane might attack one of the others.

During World War II, Haldane worked for the Admiralty developing survival techniques for servicemen trapped under water. Part of this involved him going into a sealed room and then seeing how long he could remain conscious as all the oxygen was pumped out. He wrote down every thought and feeling that occurred to him during these experiments, and it is generally accepted that his work was invaluable in saving the lives of many seamen trapped in submarines or in damaged ships. But the work gave Haldane severe nosebleeds and fainting fits, and caused a general level of ill health from which he never really recovered.

Always controversial, he was often interviewed by journalists, partly because they knew he could always be relied on to come up with something unusual or eminently quotable. Asked if he believed in extra sensory perception, for example, he said he thought it 'a gross invasion of one's privacy'. He tried to get the 'No smoking' signs taken down in railway carriages and replaced with 'No perfume' signs. Then in 1957, increasingly fed up with London, he moved to India – although the official reason he gave was that after sixty years he was fed up wearing socks! In India he spent a great deal of his time helping injured animals.

In 1965 he was diagnosed as having cancer, but wasn't in the least offended when the BBC asked if they could film him for his own obituary. During the filming there was a close-up of him doodling; what the BBC crew didn't realise was that he was scribbling obscenities in Greek! Undaunted by his illness and as brave as he had been half a century earlier in the trenches, he wrote a long comic poem called *Cancer's a Funny Thing*. He died later that year, and left his body to science.

NIGHTS AT THE OPERA

John Christie

John Christie, later to become famous for founding the Glyndebourne Festival, was born in 1882 into an aristocratic but somewhat eccentric landowning family. He was by all accounts an extremely naughty yet engaging child; at school he spent most of his time breaking windows, and was caned virtually every day either for his glass-breaking efforts or other misdemeanours. Apparently he simply accepted the caning as part of everyday life.

At thirteen he was sent to Eton but had the great good fortune, as he later described it, of coming under the influence of Dr Porter, an accomplished painter, musician and cyclist, who encouraged in the young Christie a passion for the arts. On leaving school Christie embarked on an officer training course at Woolwich, and it was here that a serious riding accident left him with a permanent limp. In 1902 he went up to Cambridge. Already noted for his numerous oddities, he became fascinated by Wagner while he was there, hammering out the great composer's work on his piano in order to evoke the passion of the music; he always had a huge towel wrapped round his head which he said he needed to catch the sweat from his exertions.

On coming down from Cambridge in 1906 he became a master at Eton, and here he was to remain, to the delight of some boys and the consternation of others, for the next sixteen years. He didn't need the small amount of money schoolmastering gave him, but he needed something to do and schoolmastering 'rather appealed'. Students who remember being taught science by him describe his lessons as totally incomprehensible, but he was much liked. His lessons were so bad that on more than one occasion he narrowly escaped being sacked.

Contemporaries talked of his prowess at cricket, a sport of which he was particularly fond. He was said to lumber towards the stumps when bowling, and at the last minute the ball would appear as if by magic from somewhere behind his head. On the football field he was described by all who saw him as terrifyingly violent, in spite of the fact that he always played in a pink silk vest.

By the time he reached his early thirties his mother had become concerned that he had not married, so she began to send him pictures of eligible women cut from the pages of *Tatler*. None quite took his fancy.

At about this time he deliberately employed a butler on the grounds that he bore a remarkable resemblance to that archetypal butler, Jeeves. Unsuccessful at getting her son married, Lady Rosamond tried to persuade him to give up teaching and become a country squire at her house at Glyndebourne in Sussex. Christie resisted and stayed on at Eton until war broke out in 1914. Despite the fact that he'd already lost an eye in a sporting accident and limped badly as a result of his riding accident, he tricked the medical officers into passing him fit for service.

In the trenches he was apparently entirely unflappable. When a soldier was blown to pieces by a shell just a few feet from Christie and his men, he whipped out a copy of

JOHN
CHRISTIE
CO-FOUNDER WITH HIS WIFE
AUDREY MILDMAY
OF THE
GLYNDEBOURNE
FESTIVAL OPERA

Edmund Spenser's poem *The Faerie Queen* and began to read from it in a loud voice, apparently in the hope – successful, as it turned out – of calming his men.

By this stage his mother was sufficiently worried about him to use her influence to get him out of the army, something which at the time it was considered quite acceptable for individuals from the upper classes to do. Back in England in August 1916, Christie's first plans for the reconstruction of Glyndebourne were drawn up. He built an organ room and extra bedrooms, and installed electricity. Then he began to employ extra staff. Job interviews could be remarkable for their brevity and eccentricity. A gardener being interviewed was asked if he could grow grapes, and when he said 'yes' he was given the job; that was the only question he was asked. Childs the butler became one of Christie's greatest friends; he was best man at his wedding, and eventually godfather to his child.

After the war ended Christie threw lavish weekend parties, spending hundreds of pounds on champagne but refusing to light fires or turn on the heating, however cold it became. Instead he always carried a small electric fire with him from room to room, simply plugging it in wherever he happened to decide to sit. He so hated to see fuel – particularly the new-fangled electricity – wasted that he frequently turned the lights out when his guests were still sitting chatting, just leaving them in the dark.

Another of Christie's interests was to keep fierce bulls, and he would climb into their fields to pet them, saying: 'They're quite safe so long as they see you are not afraid.' He still taught at Eton, and along with one or two other masters had taken up dancing. Pupils often saw him through his window waltzing with a cushion as partner.

Dining at Eton one winter evening he proudly drew his neighbour's attention to the fact that, in spite of the cold, he was wearing a thin tropical suit and no vest; and he was often seen boarding the London train with a large hot water bottle sticking out of the back of his trousers. When he got to Victoria he would unscrew it and tip the contents over the platform. In his car he always drove wrapped in a huge eiderdown.

In 1922 at the age of forty he finally retired from Eton, and the amateur operaticals that he had held during his weekend parties at Glyndebourne took on a new and more serious aspect. He had always insisted that his guests wear black tie to these events, but he himself always wore unconventional clothes – an enormous baggy suit, and slippers or tennis shoes. When he travelled to London, on the other hand, he would usually wear a top hat, blazer, flannels and cricket shoes; in winter it might be a square bowler hat, huge shapeless brown coat and tennis shoes or a top hat, spats and silk waistcoat. He invariably carried two sticks. But wherever he went, come winter or summer, he always carried one of his beloved pugs with him under one arm.

He was an obsessive eater of milk puddings, particularly tapioca, once eating seven helpings in one go. And he loved practical jokes: when driving someone who didn't know him well he always pretended he had forgotten where the brakes were; and he almost always deliberately introduced his guests to each other using the wrong names.

OPPOSITE

John Christie at Glyndebourne (Hulton-Getty Picture Collection)

Though extremely rich he always steamed off stamps that the post office had failed to mark; he refused to tip waiters, porters and bell-boys, and he worried so much about wasting electricity that he eventually employed a man just to turn the lights off in his house. When he travelled he went third class, and he refused to put locks on any of his bathroom doors. Female guests at Glyndebourne were always presented with knitting 'to keep them occupied'.

When he bought things, which he usually hated doing, he always bought in bulk. Thus when one of his secretaries needed a typewriter, he bought six; and at any one time he owned over 200 shirts. He always ordered seven copies of *The Times*, and he once had 2,000 pairs of plastic shoes made: he tried to sell them to a London store, and when that failed, thought about advertising them in the Glyndebourne Opera programme. Eventually he littered his London club, Brook's, with them. He also delighted in going for a drive to get rid of his old clothes; he would whizz along the Bayswater Road hurling grubby collars and socks into the path of oncoming vehicles. 'It's much the easiest way to get rid of them,' he would say.

If the electric light in a particular room in his house, his club, or a friend's house was too bright, instead of turning the light off he would put up an umbrella. Once in a railway carriage he got so fed up with the lights that he removed the bulbs, much to the annoyance of the other passengers.

The organ he built at Glyndebourne was so powerful that whenever it was played it brought parts of the roof crashing down, much to Christie's delight. It was far too big for the room, and although it took him a long time to accept the fact – most of the ceiling had come down by this time – he eventually decided to buy the company that made it; in fact he liked owning the organ manufacturer so much that he bought several other organ-makers and began mass-producing organ knobs because, he said, they looked marvellous stretching away before his eyes in neat rows in the factory.

As organ sales declined and he began to lose interest in organs generally, so his interest in organising operatic evenings in the old organ room increased. Eventually it was expanded into a full opera house, built because Christie had promised his wife, the opera singer Audrey Mildmay, that it would be. Within ten years it had become as famous as Covent Garden. Opera was the one area in which Christie stayed well within the bounds of the conventional; in other respects he became increasingly eccentric. When he went bald he began regularly to sprinkle rum on his head; he insisted on performing in his own operas even though he couldn't really sing, and after a visit to Austria he began to wear *lederhosen* and Tyrolean hats all the time.

His occasional rudeness was usually put down to absentmindedness, and at the worst mischievousness, because for most of the time he was a kind, generous-spirited man; towards the end of his life, for example, he fell out of bed in the middle of the night, and rather than wake Childs, his butler, he lay all night helpless on the cold floor. He died aged eighty in 1962.

'I KICK YOU, SIR!'

John Armstrong

Born in Dover in 1905, John Armstrong was a tall, stooping, wildly gesticulating, brilliant academic. He regularly recommended that his students read books in Flemish and Dutch, as if these languages were commonly understood by most students. He was famous for his outlandish good manners, and his politeness even extended to those of his students who did no work at all. He frequently fell asleep in the middle of his tutorials, and once claimed that a particular student's essay had been so long that both he and the student had fallen asleep. Many tutorials would end with students being offered a drink of terrifying alcoholic strength, though however many Armstrong consumed he seemed none the worse for it.

At a college dinner he once remarked that it would have been better if the Germans had won World War I, astonishing his listeners by then justifying the remark with the proposition: 'but think how much better our music would have been'.

He was latterly Dean of Hertford College, and when a student behaved badly he was as likely to be offered a drink as punished by Armstrong. He could, however, be made very angry indeed, even if this was a rare occurrence. On one occasion an undergraduate broke a favourite tree in the Hertford quad, and Armstrong was so cross that he kicked the young man in the shin exclaiming 'I kick you, Sir!' The phrase entered the mythology of student life, and long after its origins were forgotten by most people it was still being used by virtually everyone associated with the college.

At a discussion about preparation for German air raids during the war Armstrong was famously heard to remark that bombs falling on current undergraduates did not matter, since a new lot would soon arrive to replace them! He died in 1994.

THE UNDERGROUND BUILDER

William John Cavendish Bentinck Scott, 5th Duke of Portland

Best known for building miles of underground passageways and a huge underground ballroom at Welbeck, his country house in Nottinghamshire, the 5th Duke of Portland, born in 1800, was a gentle, generous soul. He spent a fortune employing hard-up labourers on extraordinary building tasks: like William Beckford of Fonthill Abbey (see page 109), he just had to keep building – everything from lakes and pagodas, to a skating rink and a vast stables for his string of racing horses, none of which was ever entered for a race.

He built an underground railway beween his house and his ballroom. The ballroom itself was over 170ft (52m) long with a thousand soft gas lights – far more than was necessary merely to illuminate the room – and a ceiling painted to represent a sunset. Yet in spite of all the expense, the ballroom was never used. The miles of tunnel, some running right to the edge of the estate, were probably built so that he could go about his

property without the risk of meeting anyone: making contact with people, informally or formally, was something he avoided at all costs.

When he went to London or travelled anywhere his dislike of seeing people was so intense that he had a coach built with specially low seats and impenetrable blinds; this would be driven to the nearest station and loaded onto a carriage with the duke still in it, and he would stay in it right through the journey. One of the tunnels at Welbeck was big enough to take a coach and four, and the duke would always enter his carriage in this tunnel so as not to be seen by anyone. His London home was similarly equipped in order to ensure his absolute privacy. Despite his extreme desire for solitude, the duke was evidently a generous man much loved by the thousands of estate workers he insisted on employing even when he didn't need to.

Among his other building projects were an underground billiard room and several libraries, none of which was ever used.

All those given a job on the estate were provided with a donkey and an umbrella, and no man was ever sacked just so long as he never acknowledged the duke's presence or said a word to him in the unlikely event that he should see him; anyone who nodded, bowed, spoke or even glanced at him was sacked on the spot. It was the duke's one unfailing rule. The household staff were sent letters when the duke wanted to say some-

William John Cavendish Bentinck Scott, 5th Duke of Portland (Hulton-Getty Picture Collection)

thing to them, and when he was ill he insisted the doctor wait outside his room while he shouted a description of his symptoms through the door. It is said that he had a vast collection of wigs, false beards and false moustaches which he wore when forced to walk the streets or anywhere where there was the risk of being recognised.

When he inherited Welbeck it had been a treasure house of valuable pictures, furniture, books and tapestries; by the time he died virtually every room had been emptied and painted pink. Many were also found to contain a lavatory, carefully plumbed in, but fixed right in the middle of each room. All the underground rooms were also painted pink. After his death in 1879 the pictures he had bought and inherited – some of great value – were found stacked all over the place but not one hanging on a wall, and it is believed that some time before he died he burned many pictures because he considered that they were not quite good enough for Welbeck.

Meanwhile above ground the Thoroughbred horses grew fat, and the biggest indoor riding school in Europe lay unused.

In his own peculiar way the duke was always keen on the welfare of his staff even if he could never bear to see them; for this reason he built a skating rink, and insisted that all the staff learned to skate, and skated regularly whether they wanted to or not. He gave away huge sums of money to numerous charities and he always gave money to local children and poor families.

HORSES IN THE DRAWING ROOM

Lord Berners

He dyed his doves a dozen different colours, painted pictures of his horses while they stood in his drawing-room, and built a harpsichord into the rear compartment of his Rolls-Royce: Lord Berners (1883–1950) was one of the all-time great eccentrics and practical jokers. He is probably best remembered by some for the following couplet:

Lord Berners (Hulton-Getty Picture Collection)

Red noses last a lifetime
Red roses but a day.

He lived at Faringdon House in Oxfordshire; here he erected a tall tower, and then put up a sign at its foot which read 'Members of the public who commit suicide from this tower do so at their own risk'. He also put up a sign in the grounds saying 'Dogs will be shot, Cats will be whipped'. He loved having horses in the house, and at a tea party invited one of his guests *and* her horse: this was Penelope Chetwode, also known as Mrs John Betjeman.

Berners was a generous host and a loyal friend, but anyone to whom he took a dislike would often end up as the butt of a practical joke. For example, when a diplomat annoyed him once he tied his spectacles to an opened ink bottle and a whole collection of pens and paper clips, so when the diplomat rose to make an important speech, it all went everywhere.

Whenever Berners travelled by train he hated to share his carriage, so he would wear a black skull cap and as the train approached any station where there was a risk that others might get on and join him, he would lean out and solemnly invite them in. Of course they were so terrified by this apparition that he was left alone.

Spy

THE MODERN MALAPROP

Dr William Archibald Spooner

Dr William Archibald Spooner, fellow and later warden of New College, Oxford, was absentminded, short-sighted, and the inventor of the famous spoonerism: the transposition of initial letters and other parts of words to make them ridiculous. He was born in 1844 but had reached early middle age before he began the habit that was to make him famous. It all started when he stood up to announce a hymn in the chapel at New College and he gave it out as 'Kinkering Kongs their titles take'.

He used to say he was going to London on the 'town drain', and spoke of a camel passing through the 'knee of an idol', and of its being 'kistomary to cuss the bride'. Perhaps most famously of all he referred to Queen Victoria as 'The queer old dean'; and when an aged relative visited him he told her he was glad to see her looking as 'hapless and cappy' as ever.

In his latter years he often found that the confusion of his words began to create hilarious confusions in his life; he once spent a whole day looking for the Dull Man public house at Greenwich when the place he really wanted was the Green Man at Dulwich.

He lectured in ancient history and philosophy – to the great delight and occasional confusion of his students – and died in 1930.

TRAVELS WITH MY ORCHESTRA

The Earl of Lonsdale

Born in 1857, the Earl of Lonsdale was educated privately and at Eton; he ran away from Eton, however, to join a circus. By the time he was eighteen he had given up the circus and become a fanatical gambler, and he would bet on absolutely anything; he once bet that he could walk from London to Stamford, a distance of a hundred miles, in under twenty-four hours. He did it in just over eighteen, and attributed his success to the fact that he changed his shoes and socks every five miles.

When he was at home he insisted that his family coat of arms be laid out in coloured chalks in front of his stables every day. He drove a yellow Mercedes, which initially he had returned to the factory when he discovered that it had chrome bumpers instead of the solid silver he'd ordered. The matter was quickly rectified.

He spent £3,000 a year on cigars, and whenever he travelled he took over one hundred staff with him, including a twenty-five member orchestra. If he travelled by train a member of his staff was instructed to leave the train at every stop and present the stationmaster with a five-pound note. But although he was generous he could be extraordinarily argumentative; for instance he spent five years arguing with the Earl of Derby over whether there should be an extra ladies' loo at Newmarket.

MESSING ABOUT IN BOATS

Viscount St Davids

Viscount St Davids, Jestyn Reginald Austin Plantagenet Phillips, was the second Viscount St Davids. He was born in 1917 and educated at Eton; he married three times, and at one time worked as a mate on a sailing barge. His father was already a 13th baronet, the head of an ancient family in south Wales and a direct descendant of a twelfth-century knight crusader, but St Davids set up a company to run barge trips on the Regents Canal in London. He quickly went bust. Two years later he vanished without trace after leaving his home and second wife apparently to buy a newspaper: instead he sailed to the West Indies as a deckhand on a merchant ship.

He succeeded to the viscountcy in 1938 and was eventually to sit in the House of Lords alongside his mother who was the baron of Knokin, Hungerford and De Moleys. He spoke only rarely in the house, on rather off-beat issues: the sale of fireworks and the legality of the American practice of trick or treating were two of his favourite subjects.

Famous for his eccentricities, St Davids bought a copy of *The Times* every day but never read it; instead he used it to build embankments and mountains for his model railway. His other great interest was boats, and he spent many years living on a barge on the Grand Union Canal at Paddington. He was known to local children as Peg Leg or the Pirate King because he had a pronounced limp and lacked several of his front teeth. He founded the Pirate Club which gave poor children the chance to mess about in boats. He died in 1991.

PIG FAT AND ROUGE

Lady Lewson

Born in about 1700 in Essex Street just off the Strand, Mrs Lewson – or Lady Lewson as she was afterwards known – married a rich merchant at the age of nineteen and moved to his house at Clerkenwell, then a quiet village on the edge of London.

Her husband died when she was only twenty-six, but from that time until her death in about 1800 she hardly ever left the house. Every day she made sure all the beds in the house were made up, although no one ever came to stay. She was highly superstitious: in over sixty years she never cleaned a window in the house fearing they would be broken in the process or that the person cleaning them might be injured. And she refused to allow anything to be moved in any room, believing that it might make her catch cold.

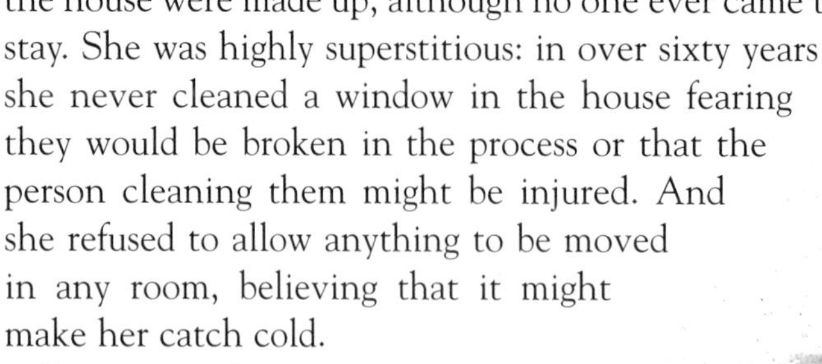

In summer she was sometimes seen reading in her garden in attire which would have been far more appropriate to the fashion of about 1690, with 'ruffs and cuffs and fardingales', and she always wore her hair powdered and piled high on her head over a stiff horsehair frame.

She believed washing was highly dangerous and would lead to some 'dreadful disorder'. Instead she smeared her face and neck with pig's fat, on top of which she applied a liberal quantity of pink powder.

A MANIA FOR COLLECTING

Sir Vauncey Harpur-Crewe

Sir Vauncey lived at Calke Abbey in Derbyshire during the later part of the nineteenth century, and was utterly reclusive; he communicated with his servants only in writing, and banished all cars from the grounds of the abbey. He also banished one of his daughters from the estate for life for smoking, and had a cousin's house in the grounds demolished after they had a row.

Sir Vauncey was an extraordinarily enthusiastic collector. He bought stuffed birds and animals, paintings, fossils and other geological specimens, swords, butterflies, shells, books, furniture, prints and vast quantities of bric-à-brac. Then, having filled a room virtually from floor to ceiling, he simply locked it up for good and began to fill another room. Little of Calke's vast collection of bits and pieces had been touched by the time his grandson Henry Harpur-Crewe inherited the house in 1981. Death duties almost led to the sale of the house and the breaking up of his father's treasures, but the equally reclusive Henry, spurred into action by the threat of the loss of a house that had been in his family since 1703, orchestrated a huge campaign to gain money from the government so that the house could go to the National Trust. Part of the campaign involved sending the great bed of state from Calke to New York where Sir Henry lay on it for a couple of days for the cameras.

The publicity worked, and the government agreed to provide sufficient funds for the house to be taken over by the National Trust.

Sportsmen and Dandies

When the leisured classes had enough money to indulge their every whim, sport loomed large in the rustic consciousness and many a man – and woman – would happily ride, drive or run him- or herself into an early grave. Squire Mytton, for example, was without doubt the maddest and most fearless sportsman who ever lived, and when he wasn't going shooting naked in the middle of January, or setting fire to himself, he drank half a gallon of port a day, and went hunting wearing a petticoat! Modern eccentric sportsmen have been known to go racing – on lawnmowers.

96

LAWNMOWER RACER

Michael Levey

Westcott, Surrey

Michael Levey is a lawnmower racer, and for over twenty years he's been a member of a small but select band of enthusiasts for what has to be one of the most bizarre of British sports. He also happens to be an expert on the rules, regulations and sundry governances, as he might put it, of a sport that started more than twenty years ago. 'It was mainly the idea of a chap called Jim Gavin of Wisborough Green,' says Michael who is scrupulously accurate about the origins of his favourite sport.

He lives in a Victorian house up an extraordinarily steep hill in the Surrey village of Westcott, a few miles from Dorking; here he plans his forays into the mad world of grass-box braking, flint and crutch guards and other Heath Robinson apparatus that make up the obscure world of fast- and not-so-fast-moving mowers. Michael is a member of the race committee which organises the serious end of the sport, and he is also a founder member of the British Lawnmower Racing Association whose key aspect is a refusal even to consider commercialism, serious competition or money: 'We don't want to go down *that* route because lawnmower racing is about fun, and the day we take the whole thing too seriously will be the day we all give up,' he says with an intense glare.

Peculiarly British – 'No one else would be mad enough to try it,' says Michael – lawnmower racing is by no means in its infancy. There are three classes or groups: in Group I, lawnmowers have to have a handler – a person running behind; 'The four-minute milers tend to win that all the time,' says Michael. In Group 2, Michael's group, the lawnmowers must have what is called a towed seat. Group 3 is for the sit-on lawnmower with wheels at front and back.

'Group 2 is great fun,' says Michael, 'because you have to know how to use your roller at the front and your grass-box to help with turning; it takes a lot of skill and can be a hell of a thing to hang on to because all the engines are souped up – though don't get me wrong, they are still ordinary if modified two-stroke and four-stroke lawnmower engines. And most of the modifications we allow – and we don't allow many – are pretty Heath Robinson-ish, although they are well made and engineered. My roller is constructed from the ends of two lampposts, the frame of my seat from lengths of old car exhaust, and so on.'

Curiously there are just three centres of enthusiasm for lawnmower racing in Britain: the area around Dorking in Surrey where Michael lives, Wisborough Green in West Sussex, and Huddersfield in Yorkshire. 'The northern and southern groups get on very well and meet every year at the Twelve Hour Endurance as we call it; that's our most prestigious race. It goes on all night, from 9pm to 9am non-stop.' The British Lawnmower Racing Association has 250 members of whom about eighty are serious enthusiasts; according to Michael, the hard core probably amounts to just a couple of dozen. In at the very beginning, Michael's first flush of enthusiasm has scarcely waned in the intervening years; and although he is now teetotal, it was through alcohol that he initially made contact with high-speed lawnmowers:

'About twenty years ago I used to drink with Oliver Reed, the film actor, and Oliver, being a bit of a mad devil himself, gave his own lawnmower to a Bill Dobson, his head gardener who wanted to enter a midnight mower race. It was a standard mower, completely unmodified which went at just two miles an hour, but Dobbo completed the Twelve Hour course and he didn't give a damn about the fact that he was going at a snail's pace with only a horse-riding hat on his head. I saw what was going on and was hooked, and became one of the inner circle – the race committee.'

Two mowers are preferred by the racing fraternity in Group 2: the Swedish Clio Regina which Michael favours, and the British-made Atco. 'The Webb is also good,' says Michael, 'but it has a rubber drive-belt, not a chain, which is a bit of a disadvantage. I've still got the blades for mine but I take them off for racing; they're a bit dangerous, as well as illegal. But that's one of our rules, we don't want people coming along with mowers that aren't really mowers so we say that a mower must have spent some part of its life cutting grass before it is elevated to racing status. Hence the club motto: *Per Herbam Ad Astra* – Through Grass to the Stars.'

Prospective racers are given a great deal of help by the club; they are sent a rule book and details on how to modify their mowers. Past fans of the sport have included Derek Bell and Stirling Moss – but how eccentric do you have to be to take part? 'I think it's fair to say you have to be pretty bonkers to want to tear around for hours on a lawnmower. But we are all mad together so it doesn't really matter. Even our official start and finish man – whose name, believe it or not, really *is* Dick Greengrass! – is a bit of a lunatic. He just turned up from nowhere one day with his wife and caravan and with a pet duck with one leg, and said he wanted to wave the flag for the beginning and end of the race. We let him, and he has turned up at just about every meet ever since; but he has no interest in the mowers.'

On average the club organises about fourteen races a season; the season is May to October, because as Michael explains they have to let the grass re-grow each year. 'You need grass for cornering when you rely on a roller or a grass-box for turning; even the roots under the mud help. Without those roots, cornering would be virtually impossible.'

According to where they happen to be racing they may have to fit silencers – 'these things make a hell of a noise at full throttle' – but that is hardly surprising, given that a half-decent Group 2 mower will reach a remarkable 40mph (64kph). 'Yes, that would be a good top speed. The record on the straight on level ground is well into the fifties, but at that sort of speed it's like hanging on to a demon!' The world speed records are held at Goodwood in Sussex each year, but other races depend on friendly landowners keen to see something a little out of the ordinary on their land. But what sort of skills does a mower racer need?

'I'm not going to tell you all our secrets,' says Michael with a twinkle, 'but we all start from a stationary position and how good you are with the clutch can make all the difference at that stage because slipping the clutch carefully will give you a smooth, graduated start. Remember these machines don't have gears, so you have to do everything from one mile an hour to forty in the same gear and it's not easy till you know how. Turning can make all the difference, too – you've got your handlebars, but the real trick is to push the front round with your feet. In the old days we didn't have brakes at all and had to rely solely on the grass-cuttings box at the front being pushed down on to the ground. Because that rests no more than three inches above the ground, it sort of slides along and you simply throw your weight forwards – well, throw the whole mower forwards really – to get some kind of braking effect. We still don't insist on a particular brake specification because that would cause arguments and all sorts of difficulties with definitions. It would be a nightmare to lay down the details.'

Once on the subject it is difficult to stop Michael, who tends to get a glazed look in his eyes whenever he discusses his favourite sport. He has been interviewed several times by astonished journalists, including a team from a German television company who spent most of their time apparently staring at him open-mouthed. 'Can't imagine why,' he says with a snort.

BRITISH LAWN MOWER RACING ASSOCIATION
PER HERBAM AD ASTRA

'Mower racing can be dangerous,' says Michael darkly, 'and there are dirty tricks that can be played, like rubbing your grass-box against another man's back wheels. We don't often go in for that sort of thing – unless we're pushed!' The sport is also extremely exhausting, and a good competitor in Group 2 can at best hope to drive for only about half an hour at a stretch before taking a rest and handing over to another team member. 'They are unwieldly beasts, it has to be said, and after half an hour you've been pretty much knocked about. If you think about it, with a seat so low you get all sorts of stones and flints flying up; it's a bit like slow castration, or it used to be till we fitted what we call flint pads to give us a bit of protection.'

Other dangers, in Group 2 at least, include turning over, going into an uncontrollable spin, jack-knifing and rearing up. 'Oh, they want to do that all the time,' says Michael with a roar of laughter. But he still sees mower racing as the pinnacle of competitive sport. 'We always say that Derek Bell only really achieved the ultimate when he won Le Mans and the Twelve Hour – that's the Twelve Hour Lawnmower Racing Championship. He's now done the double.'

The Twelve Hour track at Brinsbury College near Pulborough in Sussex is half a mile long, and it takes considerable work to get it ready for a championship. 'We're lucky, because we have lots of volunteers,' says Michael. 'There's no money in this sport, you see, we don't want money. In fact our president receives a great many offers of sponsorship and various other inducements from companies and individuals, but he always knows when they want something in return and that means we would lose control; so we always turn them down.'

In spite of the lack of sponsorship and publicity, and the devotedly amateur nature of mower racing, the Twelve Hour still attracts an astonishing 3,000–4,000 spectators who stay up all night to watch the tiny mowers hurtle round the track, their little front lights twinkling and bumping insanely. 'I suppose till they get here they can't really believe it's going to happen, it all sounds so mad,' concedes Michael.

Race procedures are taken very seriously, however, to ensure the safety of drivers and spectators: the whole track is straw-baled and double rows of ropes are set up behind the bales to keep the spectators well away from the mowers. 'Brinsbury College do all the work for the Twelve Hour race; they're great, they do absolutely everything and because the event costs very little to hold the landowner keeps all the money we charge the spectators to give to various charities.'

To avoid over-competitiveness there are no money prizes in lawnmower racing, but there are trophies. 'I've won a few, but most of them are in cardboard boxes waiting to be re-used in the future; and we don't like people putting their names all over their mowers, it's not that sort of egotistical sport. The thinking behind it is that if we can't all afford to do something – all have our names printed on our mowers or whatever – we don't allow anyone to do it. It means the rich don't get the best of everything.'

But Michael has no doubts that, in the final analysis, his sport is unusual to say the least. 'Oh, everyone who takes part is mad – well, certainly eccentric. They've got to be. We don't really want serious, sane people because that would spoil all the fun. You can always be sure that any boasting about being the champion lawnmower racer will simply be greeted with laughter by anyone who doesn't know about the sport. It's a good cure for the boastful.'

Lawnmower racing may all be good fun, but it does have its serious side, and it can even be dangerous: there are regular pile-ups resulting in the odd broken bone, and engines will sometimes simply blow up under the strain of doing what they were never intended to do; but as yet there has never been a fatal accident, though Michael remembers one rather unfortunate incident.

'A great friend of mine who was a very keen lawnmower racer had just overtaken me when he had a massive heart attack. The mower just stopped in its tracks, of course, and he was dead when they got to him. His brother told me later that that was just how he'd have liked to go.'

Lawnmower racing is definitely a family enthusiasm. Michael's son Matthew already races regularly and the racers even have their own newspaper called *The Cuttings* which comes out three or four times a season. As Michael says: 'It's quite a social sport. We meet at the Cricketers' pub at Wisborough Green on the first Monday of every month, and all the old faces turn up. And then once a year we have the Grand Grasscutter's Ball, which is definitely not to be missed!'

Even within such an obviously eccentric sport there are those who wish to scale yet greater heights of eccentricity, as Michael explains: 'At the Twelve Hour you'll get queues of people waiting to take part in Group 1 – they push a walk-behind mower once or twice round the track and then go back to the end of the queue and wait for another turn! We also have a great many people on really ancient, unmodified mowers who move sedately round the track oblivious of the fact that almost everyone else is tearing past them. I've even seen people running round the track with nothing but a lawnmower number held up in one hand!'

EELS, HIVES AND GIANT GUNS

Ernie James

Welney, Norfolk

At ninety-one, Ernie James still sets off now and then in the middle of the night from his crooked little cottage on the banks of the Delph river in the Cambridgeshire fens to set his eel hives. He's been setting them across the same river since the end of the Great War, and for the past seventy years his has been a lonely calling, because Ernie is the very last of the fen tigers: the last of a long line of what one observer long ago called a race of 'wild, untamed men eking out a precarious living catching eels, harvesting reed and shooting geese and ducks'. Even as his contemporaries began to die in the 1960s and 1970s, he bought up their puntguns and nets and carried on a way of life that had already long been something of an anachronism; for Ernie, however, the old ways are still the best and he sees no reason to give them up. 'They still want them eels and I can still catch 'em,' he says proudly.

Ernie displays his expertly-made eel hives

Even at his great age Ernie seems to have lost little of his strength. He is perhaps somewhat unsteady on his feet now, but he will still leap up at the least encouragement to play a tune on his viola: 'We learned an instrument when I was a boy because we had to entertain each other,' he says; or he will take you to see his 'willers', small, heavily coppiced willow trees. Grown in neat rows, these are the raw materials from which, like some Stone Age hunter, he fashions his 'hives' or eel baskets, the tools of his trade. Ernie is probably the last man in Britain who makes hives as part of a living tradition that stretches back centuries: he grows the willows, cuts them, strips the skin off each thumb-thick wand, and then weaves his tall, thin, stoppered baskets. These are baited with worms, and when an eel swims in through the intricately woven neck it cannot swim out again.

Eel catching, explains Ernie, was always a summer occupation on the fens; in winter the men would shoot geese and ducks using shoulder guns or puntguns. At one stage, long after most of the old gunners had gone, Ernie still kept and used four of these massive puntguns. With barrels ten feet long and carrying as much as a pound of lead shot, the puntgun is mounted on a flat-bottomed boat in which the gunner lies face down. In this position he then has to move the boat across the water, perhaps for many hundreds

PENTLAND

of yards, using only his hands as paddles, to get within shot of a raft of birds.

'It can take you hours to get in position,' says Ernie, 'and in January it used to get so cold sometimes I couldn't hardly fire the gun! But my best shot once got forty-eight birds. Friend of mine has my best puntgun now. They took some skill to use. You had to get them across the water without the birds seeing you; there might be a great raft of birds and they'd get nervous as you approached so you'd stop dead and drift till they relaxed a bit and then you'd ease yourself closer to them. One of my puntguns would take a massive charge of shot – but then she weighed nearly six stone and took two pounds of shot!'

And having handled so many guns, Ernie is something of an expert on the subject: 'I've had plenty of antique guns in my time; I used to buy them up as the old gunners died off. No one wanted them then because there was no one carrying on. One of them I was told was an elephant gun, and not more than six or seven were ever made. Would have been worth a fortune now.'

There were few other ways to earn a living in the fens when Ernie was a boy, but the James's were also the ferrymen: 'When the washes flooded, as they did and still do every year for weeks at a time, my father and grandfather did the ferrying. We had half-a-dozen boats at one time, and it's hard work rowing half a mile there and half a mile back, I can tell you! I did it for years. I used to take the postman over the flood. I charged everyone a shilling there and back. Sometimes I'd go over about ten times a day, and that's a long way when you go by hand.'

Ernie is a particularly rare survivor, for not only is he the last of the fen tigers, he is also one of the greatest. And at ninety-one he still cocks a snook at the modern world: he sticks to the old ways, ways that, by modern standards, seem decidedly eccentric. He lives just across the river from the house where he was born, and in his long life has hardly left the village for more than a week or two. But Ernie knows the fens like no other man living. He reckons his family have been fen hunters for more than three hundred years, and though he no longer catches eels quite as regularly as he used to, the lure of the river is every now and then too much for him and he will be found drifting across the Hundred Foot or the Delph on the blackest night, silently setting his baskets. In his early days, when every possible resource had to be utilised to ensure a decent living, Ernie also caught plovers for the London markets using spring-loaded nets, and these skills he now teaches to bird ringers at various local wildlife sanctuaries.

One of the greatest yet almost forgotten fen traditions was skating; in fact the fens produced almost all the great British speed skaters until World War II. This was partly because the shallow floods that cover much of the fens in winter tend to freeze readily, and in the days before purpose-built skating rinks they provided the perfect training ground. Ernie reckons that the fenmen made the best skaters because they were so fit, and 'they were fit because they had to work so damned hard!' he says with a chuckle. Ernie started on the ice at the age of three and was one of these great skaters – although every fenman worth his salt was at least a competent speed skater; it was a matter of pride in those days that everyone, men and women, learned to skate almost as soon as they could walk. But Ernie's wife's family always took pride of place among the *great* skaters.

'Turkey Smart and James Smart, both members of my wife's family, were probably the greatest skaters of all, but I was third in the Skating Championships of England in 1929 and we were always being written about in the papers. No one could match us, 'cept perhaps the Norwegians!' Ernie only recently hung up his blades, but they are still there in perfect condition hanging in his cluttered, memento-filled garden shed. They were made from oak or mahogany and steel, and simply bolted and strapped to a stout pair of boots, and were used for speed skating and for playing ice hockey.

The James' family ferry was in great demand when the winter floods arrived every year; this photograph was taken in the 1920s

'They're a bit of an antique now,' he says, 'like me, but they'd work as well as they ever did. We had no money for fancy skates then, and made our own, or as good as. Some of us had the Norwegian ones but I liked the old ones – you could stop dead on them by leaning back.'

Making the primitive but highly effective hives is undoubtedly one of the more curious aspects of Ernie's life. And as he explains, the art of hive-making is far from easy, unless you've spent the past seventy-five years doing it: 'First you've got to get your willers right. We cut 'em here when they're about as thick as your thumb and then use a rod peeler to take the skins off. Then you weave 'em in and out around your uprights. I've got them all over the world now; some on 'em's in Rhodesia and Australia. You start the hive with six-foot-long willers lying along the grooves in a special block of wood, then eleven short, splayed pieces inside for the eel to get through but not back out of. A hive will last two years, but I reckon they've been made here since Domesday.'

Ernie's rich fen accent is a rarity these days for it is relatively undiluted by outside influences. Hives is pronounced 'hoives' and willows 'willers', and all in a curious, but captivating lilting intonation. In spite of his great age Ernie still tears around the village on his bicycle, and his fame as a weaver of willow has spread so far that he now teaches basket-making to local women! But when he was weaving eel baskets and fishing them professionally, what sort of a living did he make?

'You can make a very good living at the eels. A *very* good living, because you can fish for eels in summer and fit in other things at the same time. Dredging the dykes, ferrying, and then when autumn and winter comes there's birds and fowl.

'We used a net for the plover. We'd flood a wash if we had to and then make a raised area in the middle of it and put the net by that. The plover would come to the flooded wash and rest up on the raised bit in the middle. The net was on springs and snapped over like a book when you pulled your line. You'd get 'em all with one pull and then put 'em on the train to London. The Leadenhall Market man in London would pay you.

Nowadays they get me over to the Wildfowl Trust and to Peasthorpe Bird Show in Norfolk to show 'em how the netting used to be done.' At this point Ernie leaps up and belts out a dance tune on the viola, then settles down with a cup of tea which he laces liberally with whisky. 'I generally get through a bottle a week, just about,' he says with a wink.

Ernie prides himself on being able to turn his hand to just about anything. 'That's the mark of the true fenman,' he says. 'Whatever had to be done by hand I could be put to it and I would do it. I used to cut the weeds in the river, I was in the local fire brigade, I caught moles in the winter – they're terrible here lately – and if there were a lot of ducks about I'd stop all that other work and have a week at them.'

With a dram or two inside him and the fire glowing in his cosy sitting-room, Ernie is an endless source of reminiscences, hopping from one subject to another. 'When I was young we were cut off from the world here and we knew everybody. Now they all live here but work some place else. I used to go up the pub playing dominoes, didn't I missus? But they built no end of bungalows here, and nearly all this place now is foreigners. Where's the whisky in my tea? You ain't put no whisky in it, missus.

'I played the viola and the violin on the television – got drunk, and all, while I was waiting! But we were always hard-drinking men, and there were many great characters among us; our village blacksmith was just such a one. He used to do my gun locks up. I found him once when he'd just dug three acres of sugarbeet with a handfork. Another day he turned up with a tractor and said to me, do you think you can work that old horse? And my mother was another tough one; she was 108 when she died, and about a month before she died she'd jump up and make you a cup of tea. She could skate, too – all the women could skate; but that's nothing to what they get up to these days, is it? They go wrestling today, don't they?

'I've had ten dogs, great dogs for shooting, and for years I had a cormorant as a sort of pet. He used to come every day and sit on the boat with me till the local poacher shot him; that poacher was also the local policeman! I liked that old cormorant. I used to whistle him up and I'd give him eels. We called him George. And every day I'd say "Morning, George" and he'd say "Morning!" back.'

A portrait of Ernie in the 1950s after a successful morning's puntgunning

With his violin, his massive old puntguns, eel nets and baskets, Ernie is the last link with a vanished world, and his delightful eccentricities are embodied in his continuing devotion to the pursuits of the fenmen of the past. But Ernie sees nothing eccentric about his life: he just happens to have lived into an age when the fenman has become a remarkable curiosity.

AN EAGLE IN MY GARDEN

Jack Harris

Ashford, Middlesex

There can be few people who live within a dozen miles of central London who keep a fully grown golden eagle in the garden, but one such is bargeman Jack Harris. Jack, at the time of writing fifty-five, has lived on the outskirts of the capital all his life, and now lives in one of the last few utterly rural corners of old Middlesex where it meets the great metropolis. Employed by a sand and ballast company, Jack works the barges on the extensive gravel pit that surrounds his small bungalow. The great thing about such pits is that they leave plenty of land to become wild and overgrown round about, which is why – in spite of its relative proximity to major roads, the airport and the city – this little area bears all the marks of having got stuck in a rustic time-warp. And in this unique environment Jack lives the life of a fully fledged countryman: he shoots duck from a tiny boat on the reservoir, keeps chickens and ducks round the house, and shoots foxes to feed Max, his twenty-eight-year-old golden eagle as well as his six peregrine falcons.

Jack with one of his father's prize parrots in 1949; (left) Jack and Max in the early seventies

For Jack Harris lives, eats, breathes and sleeps birds of prey. He even makes by hand all the obscure, arcane equipment associated with hawks and hawking: jesses and hoods of ancient design unchanged since medieval times, and delicate velvet-covered blocks on which his birds spend their time between hunting trips. Until recently Jack hunted his eagle on the land by the reservoirs that surround his home, but old Max is a little bad-tempered these days and Jack fears he may choose to chase a cat or a small dog rather than the rabbits that seem to be everywhere in the rough land round about. A golden eagle is a big creature, and to carry one on the fist requires a special support that also has to be carried – with boots and leather jesses or restraining leads, and a massive bird on one arm Jack looks like something from the Dark Ages.

But only the peregrines can be trusted to hunt by the reservoirs these days. Jack drives up to the Cambridgeshire fens to hunt hares with Max because of the problem of the big bird's bad temper. 'We used to train him by getting my wife to ride a bicycle along the lane here by the house with a bit of string in her hand and a baited fox-skin lure tied to the other end. The idea was that as she cycled along the meat would swing out and away from her, providing the perfect training target for Max once I'd let her get far enough away; then I'd release him. That was all very well until one day Max stopped chasing the lure and started chasing my wife!' Max has two-inch talons as sharp as razors and as strong as carbon steel, so Jack had to put a stop to these training sessions.

All around the house are aviaries built by Jack and used for resting or breeding pairs. One pair of peregrines has been kept secluded for breeding in one of these for more than two years. 'Even if they see *me* too much they won't breed, and they know me, so if they see anyone else the chances are nothing will happen. They need total seclusion, so that is what I give them. I just push their food and water through a special tube and take a look through a tiny hatch until they have bred successfully; but even with all those precautions and careful preparation, nothing is guaranteed.'

More time and space is devoted to the birds and to his working dogs than to anything else in Jack's life. His father was a keen bird man, and Jack's love of birds stems from his early days. 'My father was a great aviculturist; he kept parakeets and ran an animal food store which is when I first became addicted to birds. I had to look after the stock, but I almost can't remember a time when I wasn't interested in hawks and falcons. I had my first peregrine twelve years ago, before that I had lanner falcons, before that kestrels. I had my first kestrel when I was nine or ten.'

But Jack is the first to admit that he is lucky since he has the sort of job that allows him to give the birds the time and attention they need – which is just as well, because a peregrine has to be flown every day, and he has six of them. Falconry is also an expensive hobby, as he explains:

'It would cost £700–800 to buy a falcon today, but as I have said, I breed my own birds and I teach them to hunt myself.' The technique for hunting a falcon is fairly straightforward if you know what you are doing. You walk along with your bird on your fist (the bird wears a hood at this stage) and your dog – in Jack's case an English pointer – questing ahead of you. When it comes across a pheasant, partridge or grouse, the dog freezes and you know it has found something.

'That's when the fun starts,' says Jack. 'You remove the hood from the falcon and if all your previous training has gone well the falcon should, when cast from the fist, reach a height of several hundred feet or more. You then flush the intended quarry with your pointer. On bad days, of course, the bird will miss and then fly around for ages while you desperately try to get it back; but that's all part of the fun of it.'

Jack has the great advantage of space, in spite of the fact that he lives little more than a dozen miles from Piccadilly Circus: 'All this land around my house is owned by the water board, but it was used by the Ministry of Defence during the war years and for some time afterwards. Huge rows of lorries used to be stored here during the war, but now it's all quiet and overgrown and few people come along to disturb it. And because I am a watchman for the company I have the concession to fly my birds here.'

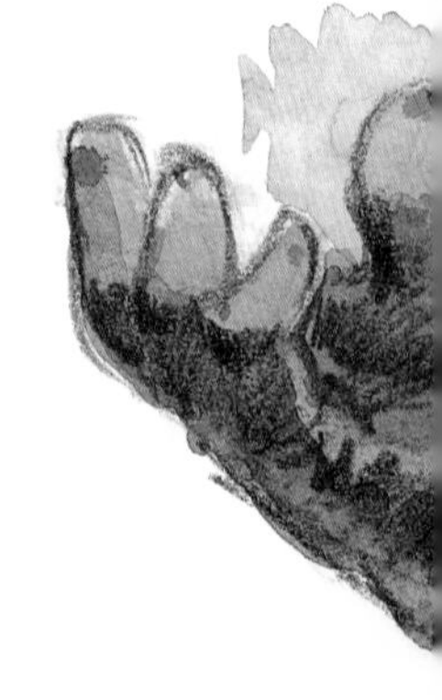

As well as flying birds and hunting them, Jack is also an expert on their training and feeding: 'Oh, feeding birds of prey is absolutely critical, especially if you fly them regularly. You see, they are like athletes – you have to keep them in trim and that means not over- or under-feeding them;

they need enough to keep them healthy and fit, but not so much that they can't be bothered to hunt. The peregrines being trained are taken to work with me every day on the barge so I can maintain that vital relationship with them. They have their own area on the foredeck, and share my cabin when the weather is bad. The company I work for has been very understanding about my addiction to my sport.'

Jack's enthusiasm never wavers, and he's a great believer in the importance of having a close relationship with his birds. 'It's not a question of it just being a good idea if you can manage it: you *have* to have a relationship with your birds – that's the secret of it. They know you well and you know them well: you're with them every day for long periods and they can anticipate your movements. This is because they have a strict feeding programme, and for the relationship to work you have to stick to that programme. The following old saying sums it up: 'A fat hawk maketh a lean purse and a weary horse', only in my case it maketh a weary Jack Harris.

'The relationship is important because sometimes the bird doesn't get back to you till it's dark, and if it can't see the lure it may well hear your voice and see a bigger target

like your head which it can then home in on and land on. I've had birds land on my head on the odd occasion in the dark, and I was glad to get them back that way!'

Like most falconers, Jack uses training techniques that are unchanged in centuries, many originating with the Arabs for whom falconry has always been something of an obsession: 'The Arabs are the originators of much that we do now with our birds. We make them do vertical jumps to reach a piece of meat, for example – this just means they have to come up vertically from ground level to your head height, but it is perfect to make them pump muscle and is very good exercise.

'These days Max is more or less retired, but in his early days he hunted the Cambridgeshire fen hares with great verve. Unfortunately his temperament has changed to such a degree that it would be dangerous to hunt with a bird of such great power; he has a six-foot wingspan and eyes like a high-powered telescope, and if something did go wrong I wouldn't be able to fly after him to sort the problem out! With an eagle, if he doesn't connect he'll perch and just keep an eye out for something else, and that used to be the time for me to have a cigarette and a rest while Max got on with it. If a hare so much as blinked within a mile radius old Max would have had him.'

But why the bad temper? 'All the old books tell you that eagles of Max's age – he's twenty-eight – become difficult and may eventually become completely unmanageable. Max is certainly heading that way, but they'll live to fifty in captivity. I feed mine on fox heads, and he loves them!'

THE MAN IN GREEN

Henry Cope

During the early years of the nineteenth century when Brighton was one of the most fashionable resorts in Britain, a familiar sight along the promenade was the remarkable Green Man: Henry Cope. He was given the name because everything he wore was green, down to the last accessory; moreover his house and coach were painted entirely green, his furniture was green, all his bedclothes were green and he apparently ate only green vegetables.

By 1806 his eccentricities had clearly got the better of him and a local newspaper reported that he had jumped from a first-floor window of his house, run to the nearest cliff and jumped twenty feet onto the shingle beach. He survived, but he never appeared again on the promenade and his final whereabouts are not recorded.

In an attempt to cure a bout of hiccups, Mytton once set fire to his own nightshirt!

THE MADDEST SQUIRE IN ENGLAND

John Mytton

John Mytton was surely one of the most eccentric men who ever lived. He was descended from Reginald de Mutton, a Norman nobleman, and for generations the family had been prominent in Shropshire. Another ancestor, Thomas Mytton, was high sheriff of Shropshire, and for his part in bringing a traitor to trial in 1480 was given land and property in the county by Richard III.

John Mytton, who was to become the most famous – or infamous – Mytton of all, was born in 1796. His father died when he was a year old, and by the time he was ten he was said by his first biographer to be 'as finished a pickle as the fondest mother and his own will could have made him'. His neighbour, Sir Richard Puleston, called him Mango, the King of the Pickles. John was expelled from Eton, Westminster and Harrow, probably a record in itself. After that he had to be tutored privately, but the tutor didn't last long either because Mytton attacked him and knocked him about so badly that he refused ever again to have anything to do with him.

He agreed to go to Oxford on condition that he would never have to open a book, and in the finest traditions of accepting wealthy students on their own terms, Oxford agreed. But even this was no good and Mytton quickly dropped out. Cambridge couldn't hold him either. At eighteen he set off on a grand tour of Europe; when he returned he married and began in earnest a life that was to cost him one of the biggest fortunes in England.

A small man, he was described by a contemporary as remarkably muscular and utterly fearless. He was said to possess 'animal faculties', and 'biceps larger than that of Jackson,

An eighteenth-century engraving shows Mytton, up to his waist in the middle of the lake, shooting herons...

the celebrated pugilist'. In 1826 he was out hunting when his hounds were distracted by shouting. He discovered a very large, very angry Welsh ex-miner who had been trying to turn Mytton's hounds on to another hare. Furious, Mytton immediately challenged him to a boxing match, and although the man was twice his size the miner gave up after twenty bare-knuckle rounds with Mytton, who made up in determination what he lacked in skill. But having beaten the miner Mytton immediately gave him ten shillings to drink his health, and that was by all accounts quite typical of the man – savage at one minute, generous the next.

Another contemporary wrote of Mytton that 'his dress would have caused the death of nine-tenths of mankind'. He always wore thin silk stockings and thin shoes so his feet were soaked as soon as it rained; nor did he ever wear a coat whatever the weather, and his waistcoat and shirt were as often as not left undone. In the deepest snow or hardest frost he would stomp through thick undergrowth or wade through lakes and ditches as if it were summer. He once lay half naked for hours in the snow hoping to shoot a goose; and on another occasion he went duck shooting in the middle of the night in his nightshirt. As a young man he would often ride fifty miles to a meet and fifty back, and he'd do it several times a week. The impression he gave his friends was of a man of almost limitless endurance, determination and strength.

He once took a coach from London to his estates in Shropshire in the company of a friend and during the journey the two men ate several hundredweight of hazelnuts. They apparently sat quite happily up to their knees in shells, which poured out onto the road when the door was finally opened. And Mytton never lost his taste for hazelnuts, or filberts as they were known then. Largely because of his wild spending Mytton was extremely popular with the Shrewsbury shopkeepers, but few did as well out of him as the nutseller, for Mytton would generally order at least two *cartloads* of nuts in a season.

Mytton owned a one-eyed horse called Baronet, and when riding home after a day's hunting he would often call at one of his tenants' cottages and ask if he could dry his horse in front of the fire. No tenant would dare refuse him, so Mytton and horse would walk in and stand by the fire for half an hour or so. And if there was no house nearby he would warm his horse by making it share a bottle of port with him. For most of his schooldays and throughout the rest of his life he is said to have drunk between five and eight bottles of port a day – and port in those days was twice as strong as it is now. If the port ran out he drank scent, or lavender water, or eau-de-cologne; he claimed the latter was excellent protection against the night air.

He loved hunting, but cared nothing for training his hounds or horses – so when times were hard he sold his hounds to the local glove-maker! His hounds were always so badly trained anyway that they chased anything and everything they came across.

Mytton is said to have owned 150 pairs of riding breeches, some 700 pairs of boots, 1,000 hats and more than 3,000 shirts. Yet when he went shooting in the depths of winter he wore a light linen shirt, no coat and a pair of dancing shoes.

Although he only lived to be thirty-eight, his acquaintances thought it was little short of a miracle that he lived so long, for it was said that he deliberately diced with death every day. He couldn't swim, but he would frequently throw himself into deep water; and he liked nothing better than for his horse or his carriage to run away with him, particularly if there was a good chance that the horse would fall and break its neck or that the carriage would overturn. He once won a horse race by making his mount swim a deep lake, even though he would almost certainly have drowned if he had fallen off. In winter he would go for long rides alone in his nightshirt and slippers, usually riding bareback. Bored in Shrewsbury one day he released two live foxes in the bar of the Lion Inn; in the chaos that followed most of the furniture and crockery was smashed.

He fought countless bare-knuckle battles with anyone who would take him on, and while hunting would force his horses at completely impossible fences. In fact if a fence was considered unjumpable they would say: 'It will do for Mytton'. In one of his most famous escapades he was driving a gig with a friend seated beside him. The friend expressed a 'strong regard for his neck', whereupon Mytton asked – caution being an automatic irritant – 'Was you ever much hurt, then, by being upset in a gig?' 'No, thank God,' said his friend. 'What,' cried Mytton. 'Never upset in a gig? Well, a damned slow fellow you must have been all your life!' And running his near wheel up a bank, he deliberately tipped them all over.

Horses were a great love of Mytton's, but when the mood was upon him he did dreadful things to them. Once, having just harnessed a horse to a gig in a horse dealer's yard, he asked: 'Is this horse any good at jumping fences?' The dealer appeared doubtful, so Mytton whipped the horse on and drove horse and gig straight at a fence. The horse got over but the gig was smashed to pieces.

But if he drove his horses hard he always drove himself harder; indeed at times he seemed quite indifferent to pain and exhaustion. He once broke three ribs while out hunting and the next day rode at the head of the hunt all day. But he never learned to control his temper, and if anything it got worse as he got older; for example a London money-lender once kept him waiting for several days, and Mytton became so enraged that he hired a team of coal heavers to knock on his door regularly all through the night. In the morning the money-lender came up with the necessary funds. On another occasion he borrowed £10,000, and immediately gave £9,000 to a friend who promptly disappeared, never to be seen again. Mytton was apparently unperturbed.

As he grew older, instead of calming down or at least moderating his mad pranks, he seemed to grow wilder and more reckless. Once, after two men had had dinner with him and won money off him at cards, he saw them to their horses, but then ran to the back of the house, dressed up as a highwayman, and galloping through the woods, cut off the two men a few miles from the park: he then held them up in time-honoured fashion and made them give up all the money they were carrying.

A horse dealer who came to the house was made dead drunk and then put to bed with two bulldogs and a bear. This same bear Mytton once rode into his own dining-room where the great and the good of Shrewsbury had just sat down to dinner. This was one of the few occasions on which Mytton came off worse, because the bear grew so cross as Mytton capered around the astonished diners on its back that it badly savaged his leg.

Practical jokes, however dangerous, made life worth living for Mytton, and the catalogue of his escapades is almost endless. When annoyed by a debt collector he gave the man a sealed envelope and told him to present it to a certain person in Shrewsbury who would pay the debt. The letter was addressed to a certain banker who was also one of the governors of the lunatic asylum; but what the letter-bearer didn't know was that Mytton had written: 'Sir, admit the bearer, George Underhill, into the lunatic asylum. Your obedient servant, John Mytton'.

When out hunting Mytton would sometimes be accompanied by his pet monkey mounted on one of his best horses; but though a lover of animals he often found himself fighting with them. And he would use his teeth to great effect: once when a savage bulldog owned by a neighbour tried to bite him, Mytton turned on his heel and bit back, sinking his teeth into the animal and lifting it bodily from the ground.

Richard Appleby, Mytton's friend and biographer, recorded that although Mytton could be savage, he was also forgiving and extremely generous; for example, throughout his life he gave the poor on his estate two bushels of wheat every week right through the year. He was said never to have told a lie – his biggest fault was probably that he would never listen to advice. When it was offered he would say: 'What the devil is the use of my having a head on my own shoulders if I am obliged to make use of yours?'

When things got very bad financially a solicitor told him that he could rescue his debts and avoid selling the family home if he would agree to live on £6,000 a year (a fortune by today's standards); but he replied: 'I would not give a damn to live on £6,000 a year'. In fact he spent a total of £500,000 in fifteen years, kept twenty racehorses and two full packs of hounds, and parted with at least £1,500 a year just buying pheasants and foxes.

He would completely wreck a new coat in one day, even if he was only going into Shrewsbury, and would wear the finest London shoes to tramp the country lanes; and every post-boy was said to lament his passing because he spent so much on post-horses

and gave such generous tips. He lost thousands of pounds, too, because having collected his cash in large sums from his bankers he would leave it lying around in his coach and it simply blew out of the windows. He would never open a tradesman's bill, and was therefore perpetually being sued; but he was so popular that no bailiff could be found to arrest him. He was forever restless, and always said that he wanted to try everything even if it killed him.

It was also said that from the age of fifteen until he died at the age of thirty-eight he was not sober on a single day. His first biographer reckoned that he was 'made mad half by nature, half by wine. He kept a bottle by him all day; and it was only when he went to brandy that his health began to suffer'. Wracked by ill-health and pursued relentlessly by creditors, in the last few months of his life, he could still be astonishingly generous. In Calais he came across a Frenchman pawning his watch for a sick friend; when the sum requested was refused, Mytton bought the watch and then gave it back to the Frenchman.

As his money ran out he took to walking everywhere, always sending his coach on ahead even in the heaviest downpour. Eventually the list of his unpaid bills grew so enormous that he was imprisoned first in Shrewsbury and then in London, where he refused all offers of help. Released at last, he was later obliged to escape to France to avoid his creditors for the second time. He died on 29 March 1834.

Thousands attended his funeral to pay their respects and no doubt to discuss his extraordinary exploits. But his hunting friends probably remembered best the day he turned up at the meet wearing a petticoat he'd stolen from a washing line; or the time he laid a spring gun which was triggered by the parson coming up the drive, whereupon Mytton ran out and accused the parson of shooting on a Sunday.

A HATFUL OF EGGS

The Honourable Mr Hastings

Born in about 1620 at Woodlands in Dorset, Mr Hastings was utterly obsessed by hunting. He had bright red hair and always wore green clothes. He built a huge rabbit warren around his house so that the requirements for dinner and supper would never be far to seek; then he built a banqueting room in a huge old tree. His large and well appointed house was filled with dogs, hawks and cats, so much so that everywhere you walked the floors were covered with the bones of small animals that the resident animals had eaten. Everywhere were hawk perches, and the chairs and sofas were always home to large litters of pups and kittens which Mr Hastings insisted absolutely should not be touched. At dinner he was perpetually surrounded by animals that climbed over and around him; and in his numerous hats, which were left all over the house, were to be found duck and goose eggs. He lived to be nearly one hundred and was still riding to hounds at the age of ninety.

HUNTING MAD

George Osbaldeston

Born in 1786, Squire Osbaldeston became the most fanatical foxhunter who has ever lived. Even before he'd finished school he was spending six days a week in the saddle, and when he bought a pack of hounds from the Earl of Jersey he became a Master of Foxhounds while still an undergraduate. He left the university without taking a degree because, he said, it interfered with his sport. He then became Master of the Pytchley, one of England's most famous packs. Osbaldeston was just five feet tall and looked, it was said, rather like a fox cub. In his whole life he took only two days off from foxhunting, one when his mother died and the other when he broke his leg.

Apart from hunting he loved racing at Newmarket, shooting pheasants and gambling whenever he could. Stories of his amorous affairs abounded; for instance, it was said that when an unmarried woman who already had two daughters by previous lovers complained to Osbaldeston that she wanted a son, he immediately told her she would have one by him – and she did. He spent every night gambling and would sometimes sit up all day, all night, and all the following day at one game of cards; having gambled away an enormous fortune he was forced to sell his estate and move to a small house on the edge of London, and it was only his wife's management of his affairs that prevented his becoming bankrupt.

He rode his horses to the point of exhaustion, and once bet that he could ride two hundred miles round the course at Newmarket in ten hours. Someone offered better odds if he could do it in nine hours, and the bet was on. On the appointed day Osbaldeston arrived at Newmarket wearing a purple shirt, white breeches and a black cap. He was still suffering from a serious hunting accident which had left him with a permanent limp, but he completed the two hundred miles round the four-mile course in eight hours and forty-two minutes using twenty-seven horses and stopping just once for lunch, which consisted of a huge glass of brandy and a small partridge.

He could be immensely chivalrous and charming, but also vicious and vindictive. As an amateur 'gentleman' rider, he knew, for example, that during a race he could crowd the professional jockeys onto the rails and the stewards would not dare penalise him for it. But for every instance of bad behaviour there is at least one that shows him in a good light – such as the time he overheard a young woman snubbed at a ball when she tried to compliment another woman on the orchid she was carrying. Osbaldeston immediately set off on a furious four-hour ride to a conservatory where he knew the orchid had been obtained. He woke the owners, paid handsomely for an even rarer orchid and rode back to the ball. He presented the young woman with the orchid and danced with her till dawn.

He once defeated the French tennis champion using his hand instead of a racquet, and when shot in the eye during a day's pheasant shooting merely carried on, not wanting to spoil the sport. To the man who had shot him he merely said: 'I told you you would hit something eventually'. On another occasion while out hunting he was knocked off his horse by another man and merely exclaimed as his assailant disappeared into the distance: 'My God! What a tailor!' He died in 1866 aged eighty-one.

A TOWERING INTELLECT

William Beckford

William Beckford was born on 29 September 1760 into one of the richest families in Britain; however, the Beckfords were also fierce, arrogant, eccentric and occasionally violent. William's great-grandfather had made the family money from sugar and slaves, but he was so bad-tempered and quarrelsome that he was eventually killed in a brawl. *His* son Thomas was also killed by a man he'd offended in a quarrel; Thomas's son, William, was the father of our hero. When he died of fever in 1770 young William was just nine years old and inherited an enormous estate: capital of 1½ million and an annual income of £70,000.

Like his grandfather, the young William was quick to anger, but he also had an uncharacteristically gentle side. In later life he was famous for his unpredictability: one minute he would beat his servants, the next give them large sums of money. But by the time he was sixty William had spent the family fortune, mostly on trying to build the tallest structure the world had ever seen: Fonthill Abbey in Wiltshire, a vast gothic complex of turrets and towers, passages and spiral staircases, secret doors, tunnels and dungeons.

For much of his adult life at Fonthill and later at Bath, William lived alone with an unattractive dwarf from Switzerland who ate only mushrooms, an obscure Italian called Franchi who seemed half confidante and half servant, and several monkeys and dogs. Beckford himself was a tall, slim man with regular features except for a rather long nose which gave him a permanent look of disdain. His youth had been extraordinarily privileged even by the standards of the eighteenth century when the aristocracy paid no taxes and paid their servants, tenants and labourers as little as they could; but even in its unorthodoxy can be seen the seeds of his later obsessions. He never went to school, and was brought up by his overbearing mother and his dominating if occasionally entertaining father. He was born in the vast, beautiful Palladian manor at Fonthill which later he had pulled down; nicknamed Splendens by the locals, it was by all accounts opulent in the extreme: the ceilings were painted by some of the foremost Italian painters of the day; every room was filled with fabulous, ornate furniture and statuary; and one vast room, the Turkish Room, was flamboyantly oriental in style with arabesques covering the ceiling and looking-glass windows to increase the sense of space.

Beckford was taught to paint by Alexander Cozens, a Russian who exerted a strong influence over the young man, introducing him to a book that was to remain a favourite for life, *The Arabian Nights*. Then in 1777 Beckford visited Geneva where he learned Italian, Spanish, German and Portuguese with extraordinary rapidity, and it was this trip that changed him from the hunting, drinking squire his father would have liked him to become. He was so taken by the cultural environment of Geneva that on his return to England, he refused ever again to hunt, shoot or fish, and for the rest of his life he called anglers and butterfly hunters torturers.

Fonthill Abbey in its full glory...

Beckford tried to make Fonthill a sanctuary for all animals. Hares would apparently come to eat from his hands, and he often said he was much fonder of his dogs than of any member of his family. Finding the local hounds hunting across his land one day he ordered a wall seven miles long and twelve feet high with iron spikes on top to be built round the estate. His mother, whom he called the Begum, tried repeatedly to get him away from his interests in art and literature and towards hunting and other traditional country pursuits, but he would have none of it; and after a sexual scandal involving the son of a family friend, any chance he might have had of being accepted as part of society was ended forever. Instead he was packed off to the continent, narrowly escaping prosecution for immorality.

By 1782 he had started writing the oriental romance that was to make him famous. *Vathek* was a tale of evil appearing to succeed only to be rewarded with eternal damnation at the last, and it was immensely popular and influential during Beckford's lifetime, inspiring work by Samuel Johnson and later Disraeli. However, the publication in 1783 of *Dreams, Waking Thoughts* led to further troubles for Beckford, primarily because the letters mocked the church and the traditional pursuits of the English landed gentry. After a further sexual scandal – no proof of which was ever offered – Beckford was ostracised by virtually everyone, and he was to be continually snubbed and ignored for the remaining sixty years of his life.

He retired briefly to Splendens, and then set out for Portugal where he was to spend a year and a half with an aristocratic, deeply religious family. He then went on to Spain

...and after the collapse of the tower

and, ever inclined to get himself into trouble, fell in love with the French ambassador's eighteen-year-old daughter, *and* with her fourteen-year-old husband *and* with his brother! By 1788 Beckford had been forced to flee to Paris, but by 1789 he had returned discreetly to Fonthill where he began landscaping the gardens on a huge scale.

Each day he rose early – he slept on a tiny narrow wooden bed which he took with him whenever he travelled – and rode round the estate followed by his dogs. He employed four cooks in the kitchen and ten footmen to wait at table – all just for himself, his Italian friend Franchi and the Swiss dwarf; no one else was ever invited. By 1795, his youth over, Beckford began planning the extraordinary house by which he was to be most remembered. He had always been obsessed by the idea of building a huge tower – the hero of *Vathek* builds one with 11,000 stairs – and, isolated but very rich, this was his chance to turn the dream into reality.

It was the beginning of an astonishing building spree that was to consume the family fortune. He employed the celebrated architect James Wyatt with whom he rowed constantly, and began work on a vast Gothic abbey; hundreds of workmen were engaged, and vastly overpaid because Beckford, uninterested in the practical details of building, thought money would be the decisive factor in getting the project finished as quickly as possible.

By 1797 the first great tower had been completed. A few weeks later during a storm it blew down, probably because Beckford had continually goaded and bribed Wyatt and his men into working faster and faster. Beckford shrugged off this disaster, however, and building started all over again. He planned to have his own coffin placed in a special room in the finished tower with a grating through which pilgrims – he was convinced there would be plenty – could view his shrine, for the new building was to be like a cathedral, a vast memorial to the greatest artist of the age: himself.

In 1800 to the surprise of almost everyone, Nelson visited the house and Beckford organised a huge reception for him. But in spite of Nelson's visit, Beckford remained a social outcast perhaps because the two men found they didn't like each other anyway. Nelson upset Beckford by complaining he'd been driven too fast in Beckford's carriage, and Beckford upset Nelson by trying to buy a peerage.

By 1807, using threats and more threats, Beckford managed to get his abbey, with its 276ft tower, finished. It was the tallest building in Europe. In the same year, despite the protests of architects, friends and relatives, he destroyed Splendens, one of the greatest classical houses in Britain; he simply pulled it down and sold the contents because he didn't think they were good enough for his new abbey. Though important in the history of taste – it was the first Gothic fantasy – Fonthill was a nightmare to live in; its eighteen bedrooms could only be reached up long, tortuous twisting staircases, and on the very few occasions Beckford had any guests they could rarely find their way back to their rooms. All the rooms were perpetually freezing even in summer, but Beckford cared nothing for the practical aspects of architecture: Fonthill was the physical embodiment of a dream, designed to shock and amaze; and it did. It also led the way to some of the greatest Gothic building of the early nineteenth century, including Barry's Houses of Parliament.

Fonthill had two turrets over 100ft high as well as the spectacular octagonal tower, influenced by the tower at Ely Cathedral; from north to south the building measured 312ft and from east to west 270ft. But what looked so imposing and magnificent from the outside was actually rotten through and through, because Beckford had so pushed his builders and architects that the workmanship was of the poorest quality. For Beckford, the attraction of Fonthill was its position high up on the downs and the extraordinary spectacle it made when seen from the long winding road that approached it.

Having built it, he almost immediately lost interest in it. He was bored with his life which was spent riding endlessly round the estate allowing no one in; it was even rumoured that occasionally he threw himself from his horse into the lake in a fit of boredom. And in the vast, gloomy rooms filled with medieval-style furniture, stained glass and monumental hangings, Beckford's loneliness must have been acute, which may explain why he had fitted the house with all sorts of curiosities; for example one door would open only when Beckford stamped on a particular spot on the floorboards; and in a room that he called the Oratory there was a full-size altar. Yet despite the luxury and splendour of the house, no one came to visit it; even Beckford's two daughters by his short-lived marriage were kept at bay in a small house in the park.

By 1822 he had entirely dissipated his fortune and bankruptcy threatened: Fonthill was leaky and uncomfortable and, as impetuous as ever, Beckford decided to sell the lot. More than seventy thousand copies of Christie's catalogue were sold and people came from all over the country to view what was known to be an astonishing treasure trove of furniture, books, pictures and other valuable objects. But at the last minute Beckford changed his mind and sold the house and its contents to a Mr Farquhar. At last he was able to pay off his huge debts, and he apparently left Fonthill without so much as a backward glance.

Then Beckford was summoned to the death bed of his former building contractor, who confessed that the great octagonal tower had virtually no foundations. In the same year, late in December, the whole tower collapsed, destroying most of the rest of the house and it was only by a miracle that no one was injured. Farquhar made the best of it and rejoiced in the fact that he now had a smaller, more manageable house in which to live; Beckford expressed neither interest nor concern. The smaller Lancaster Tower, the Oratory and the Sanctuary are all that now remain of one of the maddest houses ever built in Britain.

After leaving Fonthill, Beckford went to Bath where he bought a more modest house – and immediately built another tower behind it. Lansdown Tower rose to 154ft, nothing compared to Fonthill's tower at 276ft, but still astonishing by the standards of the day. Beckford, however, was inclined to belittle the new tower, saying that it was merely a landmark for drunken farmers returning from market. But he had built the tower at Bath and in its precise location because the countryside round about reminded him of the landscape around Rome.

From now on Beckford's daily routine remained unchanged until the end of his life. He rose early, drank a bowl of chicken soup, and then rode to his tower which was built some distance away. However, he never left the house under any circumstances if the wind was in the east. His entourage on the short journey was always the same: his steward on horseback went first, followed by two grooms carrying hunting whips, then Beckford riding and surrounded by half a dozen dogs. Finally there were more grooms carrying whips. When he reached the tower, Beckford would climb the stairs, admire the view, read for half an hour or so and then walk home across the fields serenaded, it is said, by birds and nuzzled by cattle that had grown used to him and came in the hope of lumps of sugar. Beckford's love of animals was legendary, and he grew ivy and thick brambles around the tower to attract birds.

Lansdown Tower is still there, although Beckford's landscaped grounds have all been built over. He collected huge numbers of books and paintings during his time in Bath, selling cheaply any he had grown tired of. He owned pictures by Raphael, William Blake, Thomas Girtin, Gainsborough and Samuel Palmer, and such was his enthusiasm for books that he once outbid the King of France for a collection. The house was filled with them, apparently stacked and piled in complete disorder – yet in an instant Beckford would leap across the room and select any particular one he wanted; at the time of his death he owned just under 10,000 volumes. But although he loved books in general, he hated books by women; he called Mary Shelley's *Frankenstein* 'the foulest toadstool that has yet sprung up from the reeking dunghill of the present times'. He professed to believe that Blake's poem *Tiger, Tiger* had originally been scribbled on the walls of the Bedlam madhouse. In spite of a life cut off from society – he was never forgiven for his early behaviour – Beckford himself was acclaimed as a writer of some genius when, in 1834, he published his travel diaries from nearly fifty years before.

When he was nearly eighty, towards the end of the 1830s, he still wore his hair powdered in the style of a long-vanished age. In 1842 he had a pink granite monument built next to Lansdown Tower, and it was here that he intended to be buried. But when the time came the authorities would not allow this, and he was taken, along with his pink monument, to Lynecombe Vale cemetery.

Many of Beckford's views earned him a reputation among his contemporaries for eccentricity, but if we judge from the perspective of the end of the twentieth century his ideas were in fact far ahead of his time: he maintained, for example, that medicine would one day be considered one of the most important professions, and that doctors would consequently no longer be despised as half ignorant and half dangerous (as they were in his day); he predicted, too, that aristocrats would one day marry apothecaries and cooks; and that lords and knights might marry their maids and no one think anything of it.

One of the few people other than his servants who saw him during his years of seclusion at Fonthill was a cousin of the painter W.P. Frith. For a bet he climbed over the high encircling wall and soon came across a shabbily dressed fellow carrying a potato. The stranger seemed friendly enough and eventually offered to show him the grounds and house; he then invited him to a sumptuous dinner, and finally, late in the evening, vanished through a door in the dining-room. The guest sat on for a long time until a servant said that Beckford – the 'poorly dressed fellow' – had said that since the man had found his way in, he could find his way out again, past a number of Beckford's fiercest dogs!

GOING TO THE DOGS

K. G. Gandar-Dower

Born in 1908, Gandar-Dower played tennis for Britain and loved just about every other sport imaginable, including greyhound racing which he was convinced he could make more exciting by the simple expedient of getting rid of dogs and replacing them with cheetahs. He was so convinced it would work that he imported eight cheetahs from Kenya and ran them for several years on greyhound tracks in London and elsewhere. However, unimpressed by the artificial hare they lolloped round at about 40mph – nowhere near the 60mph for which Gandar-Dower had hoped. He died in 1944.

HUNTING PIGGYBACK

Jemmy Hirst

Jemmy Hirst, a tanner from Rawcliffe near Doncaster, was born in 1738. By the age of ten he had already earned himself a reputation as a practical joker who also delighted in bizarre pranks. At school he would set up his fishing tackle and then dangle it out of an upstairs window ready to whip the masters' wigs off as they passed by below; he frequently hid their pens and ink, and once even stole the lenses out of a master's spectacles. And it was at school that he had his first taste of riding unorthodox animals: he taught himself to ride the headmaster's pig. Later in life he put this skill to good use when he started to go shooting and hunting on the back of his bull, Jupiter, with a dozen trained pigs in attendance instead of pointers. Each pig apparently answered to its own name.

Jemmy's fame grew to such an extent that George III invited him to court. To the horror of his friends, Jemmy wrote and told the king that he would have to come in a month or two because he was busy training an otter to fish. At home he lived with the otter, a fox and numerous mules and dogs. From an early age he kept his own coffin in his sitting-room where he used it as a table. On one occasion he invited all his friends round and treated them to a punch he had mixed himself – in his coffin. He kept a second-best one and invited people to try it out by standing in it. What they didn't know was that it had a trick door which only opened from the outside; once they were trapped, a gleeful Jemmy would tell them to put a penny in a slot in front of them which automatically opened the door.

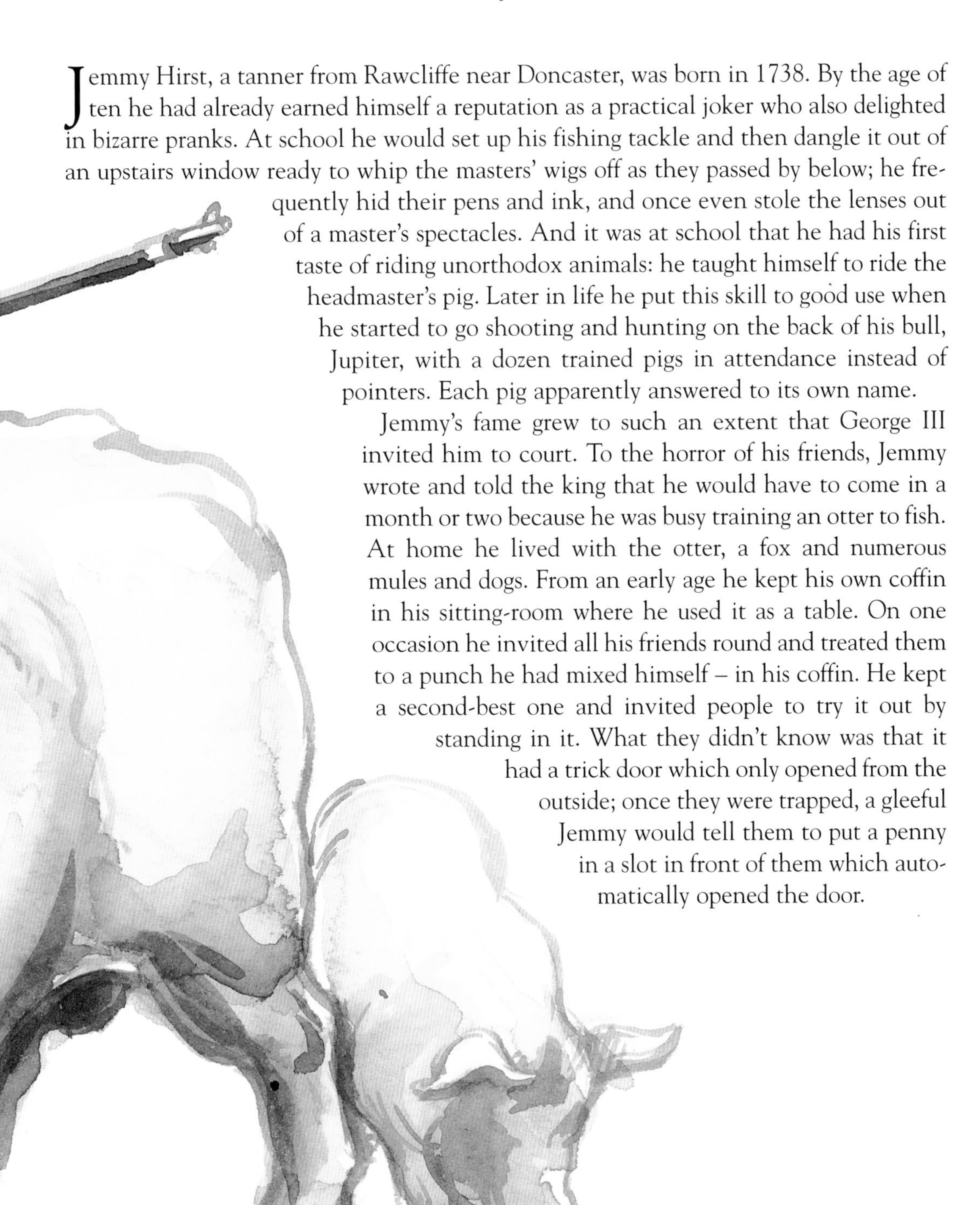

When he drove to the races at Doncaster Jemmy was instantly recognisable because he rode in an extraordinarily painted and high-wheeled wickerwork carriage, which eventually he fitted with sails. He sat in this resplendent in his waistcoat which was made entirely from duck feathers. When he placed his bets he used notes he'd made himself, and always to the value of 5½d. If his horses and mules bored him, he would harness his bull Jupiter to the shafts.

Out hunting he was always easy to spot because he wore a huge, broad-brimmed woollen hat, a red jacket with blue sleeves and bright yellow boots. He made a flying machine which, it goes without saying, didn't work, and a windmill to cut up turnips, which did.

When he knew he was dying he stipulated that his coffin be carried from the house by twelve elderly virgins, and one wonders how he must have chuckled when only two could be found.

Gardeners and Gadabouts

The green-fingered often get carried away by their horticultural creations, and few more so than Charles Waterton, who created a wildlife Garden of Eden, and who spent years alone and barefoot in the Amazon jungle; more recently, gardeners have created rustic vistas filled with life-sized statues in varying states of undress...while the aristocratic and completely dotty wanderer Edward Montague Wortley spent years walking around Europe in an enormous iron wig!

A GARDENER WITH A DIFFERENCE

Monique Huiscamp

Hailsham, Sussex

More English than the English in spite of her mid-European origins, Mrs Monique Huiscamp rides to hounds, lives in a wonderful mid-sixteenth-century house in a beautiful part of Sussex, and is a wildly enthusiastic if out-of-the-ordinary gardener who admits she knows very little about gardening. If that sounds rather difficult to imagine, the best way to explain is probably simply to say that Mrs Huiscamp likes to be different. Take her garden: five-and-a-half acres of beautiful landscaped grounds now contain a bog garden, a lake, and a full-scale authentic Japanese Garden complete with tea house and Moon Gate, the latter basically a large circular opening in a wall which allows a 'framed view' of the Japanese Garden with its large area of flat grey stones – 'they represent water,' says Mrs Huiscamp.

Elsewhere in this unusual garden the unwary visitor will come across a full-size, highly realistic sculpture of a gardener peeking out from behind a tree; in the half-light it is quite an unnerving experience to come across him. In fact he is peeking at a fat lady sitting on a log who appears to be pulling on a stocking; otherwise she is entirely naked.

Mrs Huiscamp has lived at the farm for more than a quarter of a century, and if the garden is full of delightful oddities, so too is her house. Superficially, Cowbeech looks like any other big, old Sussex farmhouse but at the back the ceilings have been taken out and it has been opened up to its original roof, and hanging everywhere from the beams and joists is a vast collection of curious bits and pieces – flags, pots, baskets, trugs, rosettes and huge quantities of antique and decorative items. This hotch-potch of memorabilia is reflected in the garden: in one corner there is a dog cemetery with a full-size dog sculpture at its head – 'Five of my dogs are buried there,' says Mrs Huiscamp; in another a life-size bronze fox creeps realistically through the undergrowth; in the front garden a giant swan takes off from the shrubbery; and elsewhere in the garden there is an orang-utang crouching ominously, staring at passers-by.

A petite woman in her sixties who wears velvet breeches and strides around her garden with the energy and enthusiasm of a twenty-five-year-old, Mrs Huiscamp says she hunts twice a week during the season, but otherwise spends much of the year in Monte Carlo or in London. She shares the farmhouse with Lord Shawcross, her 93-year-old friend, and his valet, and also her three much loved dogs; the dogs follow her continually round the garden as, here and there, she stops to pat her fox sculpture or one of her carved swans.

'Yes, I really did only come here originally for the hunting,'

The Japanese water garden

she admits. 'The rest of the year I spend here, there and everywhere.' Even after twenty-five years in Sussex she talks in a heavily accented voice.

A tall, elegant man in a long brown coat seems to disappear and reappear almost at will: he is the security man. 'Oh, he is very important,' says Mrs Huiscamp. 'With so many statues in the garden I do worry about burglars, although so far I have been lucky and have only had an old postbox stolen from the front of the house. I tried to get a licence to have a gun and the police said I would have to say that I wanted it to shoot rabbits, but I told them I wanted it to shoot burglars. They seemed to find that amusing and kept insisting that I would have to say it was for rabbits – but who would want a revolver for rabbits? Eventually I gave up the idea, although the police did finally agree that I could have my gun for shooting burglars so long as I didn't shoot them in the back!'

'My present gardener made me build the Japanese Garden after the great storm of 1987. We lost a magnificent tree at that time – it must have been three hundred years old and it left a terrible gap, and the gardener told me we should have a Japanese

Garden where it had stood. I ended up with cramp in my hand from writing cheques, it was so expensive; the green Japanese tiles for the bridge alone cost a fortune, although in fact they were less than we might have had to pay – I thought we would have to import them from Japan, but I discovered they made exactly the right thing in Ringmer which is only a few miles away.'

Mrs Huiscamp has a simple explanation for her passion for statues: 'I see something I like and I put it in the garden – why not?', and she cares for them like members of the family; she describes the special treatment required by the fat lady in the sunken garden. 'I saw her at the Royal Academy many years ago and knew I had to have her. But because she was made some years ago she is not as well made as her gardener friend and so she has to be brought into the house for the winter. We put her sitting high up on a beam in the kitchen and she seems to be happy there.'

Mrs Huiscamp's love of hunting, gardening and the English countryside suggests a keen Anglophile, and despite her protestations that she herself knows little about gardening – 'I thought flowers grew in shops' – she clearly believes that it's worth all the time and effort even though much of the garden's true value will only be appreciated by future generations. 'Oh yes, that is inevitable. It has already taken twenty-five years to bring the garden to this stage, but we have recently planted a rose walk and many trees; these plants and others like them – plants that have only recently gone in – will only be mature when we are long gone, but then that is what gardening is about. That is why I like the story of Dr Johnson – I think it was Dr Johnson – who told his gardener he wanted a row of oak trees. The gardener pointed out that it would be many, many years before his master would be able to enjoy the sight of those trees in anything like maturity, but Dr Johnson replied that that was all the more reason to plant them without further delay. And of course Dr Johnson was right – we have to think of the future, sometimes the distant future when we plant.'

Such is the unusual nature of Mrs Huiscamp's garden that it has long been part of the National Gardens Scheme, through which privately owned gardens are opened to the public. Entrance fees and money raised from the sale of cakes and tea on these days is then given to charity. 'We've always done very well on our open days,' says Mrs Huiscamp proudly. 'One year we raised almost the most money in Sussex, though we were beaten into fifth place in the following year.'

Much of her enthusiasm for the garden has developed because she is brave enough to allow her gardener an almost free rein during her absences. But when it comes to gardeners she is the first to admit that she has been unusually lucky. 'My original gardener had such vision. For example, he suggested an avenue of trees, a water garden and all kinds of marvellous things. When he died after working here for just five years it was terribly sad – although there is an interesting story concerning him. When he died his daughter asked me if I would mind if his ashes were scattered in my garden because he had loved it so much. By coincidence six trees were planted on the day he died and his ashes were eventually sprinkled over three of them. The sprinkled three flourished, the other three died. That is remarkable, don't you think?'

Whatever she discusses, Mrs Huiscamp's garden is never far from her thoughts, but she insists that she simply encourages others. 'My present gardener tends to guide me in these matters. I knew nothing, for example, about the National Gardens Scheme until he explained about it, much as he suggested the Japanese Garden. Mind you, the great thing about opening to the public twice a year is that we have to keep the garden tidy in between times; it can easily get in a mess with so much weeding continually necessary, and so much mowing – there is eight hours a week of mowing to be done alone! We have a weeder woman who comes to help, there is the full-time gardener of course, and another man comes to mow.

'A great many of our visitors come back year after year, and they often say how pleased they are to see how things are coming along and changing over the years. And do you know, they are so well behaved we never find a scrap of paper or even a cigarette butt left lying anywhere.' A disciplined, tidy woman, Mrs Huiscamp appears to be able to spot a weed from an uncanny distance, and she is understandably protective of her garden and its contents.

Her interest in gardening seems to have a great deal to do with her respect for the two gardeners she has employed during her twenty-five years at Cowbeech: 'My first gardener was paid just 7s 6d an hour but he thought it was too much, *and* he did everything by hand. I think his sort of enthusiasm would inspire anyone. Before I employed him I only used to like flowers when they were beautiful. I had no interest in, and no knowledge of how, or why or where they grew, but of course I know a little more now. I even go on garden tours to see what plants other people have and how they use them.'

It is sometimes difficult to know when Mrs Huiscamp is being entirely serious, but she clearly gets a great deal of pleasure from what she describes as her little jokes. Once when coming through customs she was asked if she had anything to declare, and told the official she had nothing except a dog. The result was consternation and near-hysteria until she explained that it was in fact a life-size sculpture.

THE QUEEN OF COURSING

Irene Peeling

Wentworth, Cambridgeshire

The front of Irene Peeling's house is solid, yellow brick Victorian, the middle section bears all the marks of eighteenth-century craftsmen and jobbing builders, and at the back is the low-ceilinged, cosy, original farmhouse which, with its crooked walls and heavy beams, might be five hundred years old. Mrs Peeling, now eighty-four, seems almost to curl up into her house like a cat in its basket, so well does she fit inside its cosy, cluttered interior; she is usually to be found by the fire in the big old kitchen. An eighteenth-century grandfather clock ticks quietly in the hall, and all around, virtually covering the walls, are pictures of greyhounds, famous dogs from the early years of this century, dogs trained by her father, her uncles, her grandfather and great-grandfather. And there are also the dogs she has reared, including several for the greatest of all coursing events, the Waterloo Cup.

This is all part of an enthusiasm bordering on fanaticism that takes Mrs Peeling back through four uninterrupted generations. Her whole life has been taken up with dogs, particularly with greyhounds and the hunting of the hare. She is a fund of good stories too, all delivered in an intense, lilting Cambridgeshire accent and punctuated by visits to various parts of the big rambling house to collect

objects, papers and artefacts that help illustrate her story. She moves around with a rapid, sideways-glancing walk as she leads you from one precious collection of objects to another. Coursing has been central to her whole life, but she doesn't see hare catching as the purpose of the sport. To think of coursing as a means to catch hares is entirely to miss the point, she maintains: the whole aim is to test the skill of the dogs.

'Coursing is really watching and judging the skill of a running dog. It was always the sport of the fens, and it's been the love – some might say the obsession – of my life. My family has always trained and raced greyhounds, probably for much longer than any of us could even guess.' And these greyhounds weren't just pets and sporting dogs; they had almost human characteristics. The best dog the family ever owned, called the Artful Dodger, is a case in point, as Mrs Peeling explains while trying to demonstrate the use of the coursing leash, a complicated contraption of leather and brass that allows two greyhounds to be released at precisely the same moment.

'My uncle owned Artful Dodger, and because they lived in a sleepy, quiet village – well, they were all sleepy quiet villages then, at the turn of the century – he saw no need to lock the Dodger up. That dog always wandered about the place as much as he liked, and he was so brainy he was soon into everything. At that time there was no such thing as school dinners, so each child would take some sandwiches in a bag and hang the bag in the school cloakroom while the morning lessons went on. Well, Dodger discovered this and he would sneak into the school by some crafty means, find his way straight to the cloakroom, pull down a child's bag and help himself. My grandmother used to say there wasn't a day when a boy didn't come to the door and say, "Mrs Cross! Dodger's had my lunch!" She'd always have them in straightaway and make them something; and the children were never upset; they all thought it was a great joke and knew that all would be well because my grandmother was always there to help.

'Helping other people and knowing everyone in the village was the way things were then. My grandmother was known as the "district nurse" even though she wasn't anything of the sort because if anyone was ill or in trouble she'd put on her black shawl and her bonnet and set off to help, whether it was a woman in labour or a sick child. All that comradeship has gone now.'

A tiny, energetic woman, a little bent now under the weight of her years, Mrs Peeling is nonetheless bright-eyed and full of enthusiasm. She has fiercely resisted efforts to move her out of her big old house, and she refuses to accept that a time may come when being out in the worst winter weather at a coursing meet will be beyond her. Indeed she seems to become twenty years younger when the conversation veers back, as inevitably it does, to greyhounds:

'They are such marvellous animals, but to understand *why* they were so important to us in this part of the world you have to spirit yourself back to when it all started – look at that picture of my uncle and the Artful Dodger in 1902. No one had vans or cars then, no one had the means to go anywhere, we weren't like you modern people rushing up and down the countryside in motor cars the whole time. All our coursing was between neighbours and friends. No one travelled for their sport, and all the sport and entertainment local people had was coursing and playing cards and dominoes, while the women sang and played the piano.

'For a coursing match in those days they'd just put a ten-shilling note down and have a run; the villagers ran their dogs against each other, and in that respect the sport has lost some of its charm because it's all much more professional now – the great characters have all but gone, and many people we don't know come from all over the country to compete with our local dogs. When I was a girl all the villagers went everywhere on foot, and though the farmers and landowners had upstanding horses to ride, people generally travelled to a meet only so far as they could get with a pony cart, say half-a-dozen miles or so.'

Coursing has always been one of the great fenland sports – along with skating and shooting – and it has inspired characters like Mrs Peeling whose lives became tied up with it almost to the exclusion of everything else. In fact, so embedded in the fabric of local life was coursing that when Artful Dodger won the Quanea Cup in 1902, the local parish priest wrote a poem to celebrate the great victory!

The Peeling family's devotion to coursing is evident from the inscriptions on trophies all around the house. Irene has lived in Wentworth for fifty years – although it isn't ideal coursing country, as she explains:

'No, it's not very good at all, but a little to the east of here, where you are in the fens proper, it's great country, good and flat with rich black soil, not heavy clay. Long ago – and I'm talking about the end of the last century and earlier when many of my photographs were taken – the fens weren't just swarming with eels, they were swarming with hares as well because *we didn't have the chemicals*, you see, the terrible agricultural chemicals, and with so many hares we had such great matches. In those days they were held every single weekend.'

Apart from coursing there is only one subject that inspires Mrs Peeling: the hare. Like many fieldsports' enthusiasts, she sees no contradiction between a great affection for the hare and a love of hunting it, and explains that essentially it is the competition between dog and dog, and not between dog and hare, that matters: 'On a typical day as many as thirty hares might be chased, but we would be very lucky to catch more than two or three, very lucky indeed. What people forget is that coursing people take great delight in watching their dogs chase a hare, but they cheer when the hare gets away. And we *never* leave a hare wounded in the way shooting people do – a greyhound will either kill the hare instantly, or it will get away safe.'

Mrs Peeling is utterly devoted to her sport and to the two animals on which it depends. An expert on the hare, its habits and habitats, she is also a severe critic of those she sees as the real enemy: 'Modern farming practice has done away with a great many of the hares because the sprays kill the leverets – lying on the surface as they do they are hopelessly vulnerable. A mother hare's way of keeping her babies safe is to leave them out in the open and sleep away from them – that may sound remarkable, but if she were to be seen with them, although *she* might be able to get away quickly in the event of trouble, they would have no chance. So she puts them where nature and a million years of caution tell her to put them; she herself, some way off, can put on a fair

old speed and lead danger away and escape. Hares always remember where they've left their young, that's one of the marvellous things about them. That old hare will lie out with her ears to the ground and pick up every sound long before you do.

'Foxes get 'em, of course, and shooters, but personally I don't think there's anything clever about shooting a hare – they stand high on the land so there's no art in it, and many times they are just wounded and crawl away to die a slow death; so I don't think much of those who go in for that sort of thing.' As she warms to her subject Mrs Peeling grows ever more enthusiastic, bobbing up and down to reach for cups, vases, pictures, photographs and countless other mementoes, each inscribed to a great greyhound from the past.

As well as being an expert practical courser she is also an authority on its history. She remembers how coursing, one of the world's oldest and least known sports, only developed gradually from its early unregulated days and that it was some time before it obtained, at last, a set of rules and regulations. Her family, not surprisingly, were coursers long before rules were ever heard of: 'Until 1902 we did whatever we liked. In that year the rules of affiliation to the National Coursing Club were laid down, but my club, the Isle of Ely Coursing Club, started by my ancestors, is far older than that. It's one of the oldest in the world. I think the Swaffham Coursing Club might be the only club that is older.'

At this point Mrs Peeling leads the way out through the old kitchen into the yard to show me a delicate, prancing, brown and white greyhound: 'I only keep her as a pet now; she's too old to run. But greyhounds make marvellous pets, very quiet, obedient and very clean. My father thought they made the best pets of all and he knew a lot about dogs. And I've had hundreds of greyhounds in my life, as well as rearing a great many puppies for other people.'

According to Mrs Peeling the whole secret of a good dog is in the rearing. A puppy must learn to use its brain and its lungs, she says, and it needs plenty of exercise – and vegetables. When it comes to greyhound puppies Mrs Peeling is absolutely convinced that a fairly hefty quantity of vegetables is the best thing: 'Making a good dog is just a question of running miles over the fields with it every day, massaging it regularly and giving it plenty of good food. People don't believe you when you say "massage and vegetables", but they are both very important. Absolutely vital. We've all got secret diets for our dogs, too – and I'm not telling you mine! But plenty of green vegetables, that's a great part of the secret, especially for puppies, together with a goodly amount of red meat and very little fat. They must be allowed to run loose, too, as much as you can let them because they're like athletes. If an athlete doesn't exercise his limbs he'll lose the best use of them, so the more he runs the better he is at it – and it's the same with dogs.'

Filled with many happy memories of her great triumphs and her favourite dogs, Mrs Peeling's only real regret is witnessing such drastic changes in the countryside: 'We didn't have cars long ago, but there were so many of us on the land and the farms were always busy. Now, everywhere seems empty because farming just doesn't need the numbers of men it once did. And when there were lots of people about there were lots of coursing dogs, of course, so that was altogether much better!'

Soon we are back on her favourite subject, and digging excitedly through bags of documents she comes across a meet card from nearly fifty years ago; immediately it prompts a lively dissertation on the physical characteristics to look for in a greyhound: 'When you're choosing a dog you look for a deep chest, a long tail and a broad back. The tail is most important because it's the ship's rudder so to speak, and when a greyhound is running at top speed it's the rudder that stops it falling over. A greyhound hunts like no other dog because it doesn't rely on scent at all, only sight. Nine times out of ten a dog will over-shoot the hare during a course because the hare will stop dead and the dog can't. Then the dog has to come back at the hare, by which time the hare has had a very good start and is usually long gone. Points are given to each dog according to how well it turns.

'All competitions are eliminators; so if your dog wins its course, it is then paired with another winner for the next round. The hares have a big advantage over the dogs because they know the land – they were born on it, after all. The old hare knows every nook and cranny.'

Mrs Peeling has no plans either to slow down or to retire from coursing. Indeed she is, by her own account, almost more enthusiastic now than she has ever been. 'I'm always out coursing! I never miss a day from October to 7 March each year when the season ends. I wouldn't miss it for the world because it's the greatest sport there is.'

TRAVELLING TAXIDERMIST

Charles Waterton

Charles Waterton (1782–1865) was the twenty-seventh lord of Walton Hall in Yorkshire, ten miles from Wakefield; at eighty and nearing the end of his life, he was variously described as looking like a spider after a long winter's hibernation, or like someone recently discharged from prison. He wore such shabby clothes that he was often mistaken for a vagrant or a farm worker, and visitors who asked him for directions to the lord's house would often offer him a penny, which delighted him. On formal occasions he would wear a dark blue, brass-buttoned, swallow-tailed coat that was almost a hundred years out of fashion. It was the coat he'd worn at school. Visitors to Walton Hall who rose early frequently spotted him running about his heavily wooded estate barefoot, stopping now and then to climb a tree at astonishing speed.

Charles Waterton with stuffed bird and bodyless cat

All Waterton's clothes were threadbare and curiously stiff because he continually immersed them in biochloride of mercury, a substance he used to protect his specimens of natural history from the ravages of moths, mites and bad weather. To the astonishment of neighbouring farmers and landowners he refused to chop down trees on his estate, however old or decayed they might be, because he believed – quite rightly – that they provided an excellent habitat for birds and insects.

In fact Waterton was so fascinated by birds and animals that he often sat for hours at the top of a tree to stare at an owl or to stroke the feathers of a particular bluetit that had grown so used to him that she had lost all fear. In an age when the rarer a bird or animal the more likely it was to be shot, Waterton refused to allow any bird or animal on his three-hundred-acre estate to be molested in any way.

He once described in a letter to his sister how, on the long road from Walton Hall to Leeds, he had seen neither a bird nor an animal of any kind – they had all been shot or trapped by the local people and it was only in his own grounds that the sound of bird-song could be heard. But if the park was packed with birds and animals, the house itself was even more densely populated by specimens of wildlife and natural history, collected by Waterton during his travels as a young man in South America, only these tended to be stuffed or preserved in a number of different liquid concoctions for which only Waterton had the recipe. These included gorillas, monkeys, rare birds and even a full-size crocodile.

But Waterton was always full of surprises. Half-way through dinner, for example, he might decide to stand on his head. Or he would demonstrate, usually to distinguished visitors, the benefits of being double-jointed by sitting through most of dinner with his foot firmly wedged behind his ear. Waterton's eccentricities made him famous in his own lifetime, but he was also famous for his achievements, most notably the publication in 1826 of his *Wanderings in South America*. His private park, with its long, meandering, thirty-acre lake and its vast number and variety of animals, also added to his fame because it attracted thousands of visitors each year – and this at a time when the most common reaction to a rare animal was the desire to shoot it.

Waterton's book about his travels revealed to an astonished public that he had spent years in unknown jungle, sometimes spending months at a time entirely alone. He had survived without shoes, guns or any European aids, and as a result of his researches he had developed a fascination for and a huge store of knowledge about rare species of birds, plants and animals. In order to preserve the specimens he collected on his travels Waterton taught himself the art of taxidermy; in fact his work in this field is generally recognised as superior to that of the taxidermists employed by museums up and down the country at the time, although his precise techniques were never written down or explained to anyone.

Tall and very thin with close-cropped hair, Waterton always appeared to be concentrating intensely. He spoke with a heavy Yorkshire accent, but was self effacing, polite and always charming to visitors, many of whom knew him only from his book and assumed that, having spent so much time in the wilds, he would himself be rather wild. In the entrance hall and throughout the numerous rooms of his big eighteenth-century house stood the stuffed animals, head-dresses, spears, boxes, chests, feathers, skins and paintings he had collected on his travels. But though a serious naturalist, Waterton was also a bit of a joker. For example, some of his taxidermist creations were deliberately designed to fool the gullible and provide a bit of amusement for Waterton; his most famous was called the Nondescript, a goblin-like creature made from a howler monkey's bottom, but given piercing little eyes and a curious, almost grinning mouth!

Waterton's Nondescript

When showing visitors around the house Waterton would occasionally spring up and swing for minutes at a time from the richly carved door frame; friends who visited the house regularly got quite used to seeing him there, testing out the techniques of the monkeys he had spent so long studying. But at the heart of his eccentricities, at least as far as his contemporaries were concerned, was his tolerant attitude to animals. He was a passionate conservationist long before such a thing was considered either sensible or respectable – anyone who treated animals as he did had to be mad.

As devout Catholics, Waterton's family had long been kept out of the centres of power in spite of their ancient lineage. Waterton's father had been fond of telling his son the fable of the black and brown rats: the brown or Hanoverian rats had come to England and pushed out the black rats, much as the Protestant Hanoverians had pushed out ancient Catholic families like the Watertons. This is why, in spite of his enthusiastic protection of virtually every bird and animal, including the black rat, Waterton nevertheless waged a fierce and unremitting war against brown rats in and around Walton Hall.

Waterton came from a long line of fairly dotty individuals. His mother frequently behaved outrageously; on one occasion she was stopped at a toll because she had three horses pulling her carriage instead of the regulation two – she argued vociferously with the toll keeper, however, swore at him and turned back home where she put three oxen in the shafts – she then returned to the toll gate and had to be allowed through.

At his first school, Tudhoe, Waterton was repeatedly and severely beaten for collecting and keeping animals, insects, and birds' eggs. But things improved when he moved from Tudhoe to Stonyhurst, a Catholic school in Lancashire. Within just twenty miles of the coast and surrounded by unspoiled countryside, Stonyhurst had the advantage of having staff who were far more sympathetic to Waterton's unorthodox enthusiasms. Stonyhurst was the family seat of the Catholic Shireburns and had become a school in 1794; Waterton arrived just two years later and stayed for five years, but his fondness for the school continued for the rest of his life, which may explain why he insisted on wearing his old school coat until the day he died. Waterton's masters at Stonyhurst realised that his interest in natural history would be better encouraged, not punished, and it was this which cemented his undying love for the place. Indeed one of his teachers, Father Clifford, remained a close friend until the end of Waterton's life.

His friendships with men like Clifford were matched only by his growing fascination for wild creatures and their habitats. Much later in his life, Waterton's neighbour Sir George Pilkington proudly showed him a raven he had just shot; he was particularly pleased because he thought it was probably the last raven in Yorkshire. Waterton was furious and denounced Pilkington to his face as a scoundrel. In his *Essays in Natural History* published in 1840, Waterton wrote, 'I despair of ever again seeing this fine British bird in any of our woods'. The unthinking destruction of wildlife was something he could never accept.

Happy, fulfilled and eager to spend his life studying animals, Waterton left school in 1801; however, because of the institutionalised discrimination against Catholics – they were not permitted to enter a university – he had to continue his education abroad. In 1802 he set sail for Spain and a series of journeys which, with only a few breaks, were to last for almost twenty-seven years. In Malaga he caught yellow fever and, astonishingly, survived; he found subsequently that he was immune to the disease and could walk without further risk to himself through the terror-stricken people, 'like Dante among the dead'. He believed he had become a charmed, almost magical figure.

When the yellow fever epidemic was over he was allowed to leave the country; then, after a very brief return to England, he set sail for his father's sugar plantation in British Guiana, then considered well beyond the limits of the civilised world. Here Waterton was one of the first Englishmen to study the deadly poison, curare. He explored the little-known interior jungles, caught malaria, mixed his own purgatives in an attempt to cure himself, frequently let his own blood – and studied the vast exotic array of plants and animals. By 1812 he had so toughened to the life that he gave up wearing shoes and learned to find his way through the jungle and climb trees like a native Indian.

Then in 1812, aged thirty, he set out on his first lengthy tour of the vast interior where few if any Europeans had ever ventured. Many considered such a journey tantamount to suicide – no European would be able to withstand for long the parasites, diseases and poisonous creatures endemic to the jungle. But stubborn, determined and

Walton Hall: the view across the lake

enured to hardships, Waterton set off – and in the rainy season, without doubt the worst possible time. He journeyed for three months and returned with numerous previously unheard-of specimens; but he was also racked by malaria which continued to affect him for the rest of his life. On a later journey he caught a tiger cat, tamed it and took it back to Walton Hall where it developed a great talent for catching rats.

Back at Walton Hall in 1813, Waterton spent three years restoring and repairing the family home and park: life in the jungles of South America had taught him mercy and the value of animal life, he maintained, and indeed it was this attitude that coloured everything he was to spend the rest of his life trying to achieve at Walton Hall. He quickly noticed that the local poachers, gamekeepers and sportsmen were in the habit of shooting just about anything that moved and as a result had destroyed virtually all the local wildlife. Immediately he began the long, slow process of encouraging birds and animals back: he built nests for owls, and kept half-decayed trees propped up by poles for them and for other birds; he then threatened to strangle his keeper if ever he molested any bird or animal on the estate.

Within a few years the skies around the hall were filled with birdsong again, and many animals that had long been absent began to reappear. It was at about this time that Waterton began climbing his own trees; he particularly enjoyed sitting at the top of a big oak and reading Ovid's *Metamorphoses*.

Fascinated by curare, quantities of which he had brought back from South America, Waterton demonstrated its extraordinary properties many times. He once used it to knock out an ass for the benefit of the Royal College of Physicians. Its lungs were then inflated artificially for two hours until the curare wore off. It then awoke and was none the worse for its experience. In fact Walton took it home and it lived at Walton Hall for a further twenty-five years.

Ever restless, Waterton set off once again in 1816 to explore the jungles of South America. He wandered through Brazil, Surinam and Guiana, but he found it impossible to organise a journey deep into the interior and eventually ended up in the familiar territory of British Guiana. This time he was so moved by the plight of the native indians that in 1817, through his Jesuit friends at Stonyhurst, he managed to arrange an audience with the Pope to discuss the matter. However, having arrived in Rome he climbed to the top of a statue in the Vatican and left his gloves there as a memento. The Pope was not amused and Waterton's audience was cancelled.

Despite this disappointment he made good use of his time in Rome, for he noticed that a garden he was in the habit of visiting each day was always filled with an extraordinary number of birds of every variety; what seemed to attract and keep them in the garden was the vast amount of dense ivy that covered the statues and trees. As soon as he returned to England Waterton began to plant ivy all over the gardens at Walton Hall.

In 1819 he set off for his third and final trip to South America. So toughened was he by his experiences that he had learned to control his recurrent bouts of malaria, and he was able to carry out many experiments on himself. He allowed flesh-boring insects to dig into his hand, for example, while he watched them and took notes; he also ate howler monkey and turtle eggs and wasp grubs – anything and everything in fact that he'd noticed being eaten by the native Indians. His experiments were all meticulously recorded in his notebooks. If he fell ill, as he frequently did, he simply watched the effects of his ailment as if it were all happening to someone else. His enthusiasm for experiment sometimes brought only disappointment however: in spite of sitting out in a likely place night after night, for example, a vampire bat never came to drink his blood.

Among the notes he took there are some strikingly modern and, even by our standards, perceptive comments. He was one of the very first naturalists to notice, for example, that animals – whether snakes, tigers or toads – never attack humans for the sake of it, but only when they feel threatened. This was a novel idea at a time when it was believed that animals attacked humans because they were somehow uncivilised, part of brute creation. Waterton was therefore able to observe some of the world's most deadly snakes simply by sticking to the rule that if you approach them carefully they will not harm you. However, when he wanted a specimen he could be ruthless, once catching a huge boa constrictor alive and tying its mouth with his braces. On another occasion with a smaller boa constrictor that he estimated could not quite crush him to death he simply picked it up and walked along with it coiling round him and squeezing him: 'He pressed me hard but not alarmingly so,' he wrote in his journal.

Waterton's most famous exploit occurred during this trip. Eager to obtain a crocodile

(or 'cayman' as he called it), he offered money to anyone who could secure one for him. A native used a crude rope fishing line baited with a rat and managed to hook one of the giant reptiles; he then sent a message to Waterton saying he had secured the animal. What he didn't say was that it had been hooked but was still very much alive – and very angry – at the end of the rope; half-a-dozen natives were needed just to keep it near the bank of the river. When Waterton arrived the crocodile was thrashing around in a couple of feet of water, but none of the locals would go anywhere near it. Using a small boat Waterton approached the animal and then, to the utter astonishment of all, leapt on to its back. The crocodile apparently went berserk, as Waterton recalled in what was to become his most famous book, *Wanderings in South America.* With his usual remarkably cool approach to danger, he related the capture: 'The people now dragged us about forty yards on to the sand. It was the first and last time I was ever on a cayman's back. Should I be asked how I managed to keep my seat, I would answer I hunted some years with Lord Darlington's foxhounds'.

Waterton had a considerable reputation as a prankster, and this affected attitudes to his book *Wanderings in South America*; it was rubbished by his detractors who accused him of making it all up. In some respects he undoubtedly was his own worst enemy because he just couldn't resist a practical joke, and the pranks for which he became famous meant that many people refused to take him seriously even when he really was being serious; and many found the episodes described in *Wanderings* difficult to believe simply because the facts of life in the South American jungle *were* at that time so unbelievable. The book did eventually become a bestseller with the public, but not with the scientific establishment who disliked the author and were, in Waterton's view, far too self-important. He felt they just couldn't take a joke and couldn't be bothered to separate the genuinely scientific content of his work from the humour.

Waterton himself enjoyed his reputation as a joker because he used his practical jokes to revenge himself on people who had annoyed him. For example, the Nondescript (made from the monkey's bottom) was apparently modelled on the features of a tax inspector in Liverpool who had impounded Waterton's specimens on his final return from South America! In more serious vein, official attitudes to his specimens so infuriated Waterton that he gave up all plans to show his collection or to lecture about his travels as he had originally planned. Largely because of this his life at Walton Hall became increasingly isolated, and he himself more belligerent.

After he returned from South America in 1826 he had a high wall built right round his estate; this was partly to keep his animals in, but mostly to keep the public out. It cost £9,000, a colossal sum by the standards of the time, but he claimed he could afford it because he never drank wine. And while the rest of Yorkshire shot and killed every bird and animal that moved, Waterton encouraged every living thing to take sanctuary in his three hundred acres. Herons, always easy prey to the gun, came in large numbers, along with the much-persecuted kestrel; dozens of owls could be seen about the place, together with hundreds of virtually tame hedgehogs. Waterton gave sixpence for every live hedgehog brought to his gates. Hares were among the few creatures that never thrived in the park; perhaps the all-enclosing walls made it too restricting for them.

At about this time Waterton decided, almost out of the blue, to marry the daughter of a friend whom he had met during his travels. Charles Edmonstone, long a resident of British Guiana, had married a native woman, and Waterton married one of their children, Anne; he brought her to live at Walton Hall in 1829. A year later she gave birth to a son, Edmund; two weeks afterwards she died, and Waterton never really recovered from the loss, believing that he was in some measure responsible. After Anne's death Waterton looked after her two sisters who came to live permanently at the house.

As the number of birds and animals in the park increased, Waterton had a big telescope fitted in the middle of the drawing-room so that he could watch them. Staring through the lens he would often pause to express his frustration at the fact that he could not explain to the birds that it was dangerous to stray beyond the walls of the park. He grew very fond of particular creatures, such as the bluetit that nested at the top of a fifty-foot ash tree; he used the skills he had learned in the jungle to climb up every day to see how she was getting on. He spent much of the rest of his time dashing barefoot across the lawns in pursuit of various animals which he would catch and pick up, examine and then release, and he would regularly invite groups of lunatics from the local asylum to look round the house and park. He told his friends that they were far more likely than anyone else to appreciate his work.

After the death of his wife he stopped sleeping in his bedroom and moved to the unheated attic where he slept on the bare floorboards covered only by a thin cloak. He was to sleep here for the rest of his life. For a pillow he always used a solid piece of carved wood, and he often got up at three in the morning to write, sometimes to climb trees or to work on the preservation of some specimen he had obtained. Around the house, now liberally decorated with old masters brought back as a job lot from a collector in Germany, Waterton began suspending his preserved specimens from the ceilings: everywhere were swaying birds, mammals and reptiles. Jumbled together in heaps and piles, in corners and in display cases were masks, spears, horns, war clubs and hunting whips, poisoned arrows and blow pipes, stuffed hippos, gorillas and monkeys. The house was a source of continual wonder and astonishment to those lucky enough to be invited inside.

Eventually Waterton opened the park to anyone who wanted to visit it; 17,000 people came each year during the 1840s. He charged no fee and stipulated only that no one should come in with dog or gun. Few visitors would have believed that the ragged, often shoeless wizened man wandering about the estate was in fact the owner.

Much of Waterton's adult life was taken up with battles with a local factory where soap was made. Fumes from the factory chimneys damaged trees in his park and polluted a local river, but because conclusive proof of damage was extremely difficult to obtain, it cost Waterton a fortune to obtain only a partial victory.

Throughout these years he ate only the simplest food: breakfast invariably consisted of a piece of dry toast and a cup of hot water; lunch was always bread and watercress. It was said by a friend that Waterton ate just about enough to keep a blackbird and two white mice alive. During Lent each year he stopped eating altogether except for black tea and dry bread. He told a friend that this diet cleared his head and his intellect and though he was nearing sixty enabled him to walk fifteen miles in a day without fatigue and to climb trees like a youngster. As he grew older his style of dress became increasingly bizarre and shabby. On the rare occasions he visited the houses of aristocratic friends and acquaintances, the servants invariably thought him too down-at-heel to be anyone of importance, and took him to the kitchens until someone upstairs could vouch for him. Waterton thought this a huge joke.

At the age of eighty he was still climbing sixty-foot trees with his pockets full of nuts, berries and other titbits, and he would still show visitors how he could scratch the back of his head with his foot. His conservation campaign continued unabated; for example, when he realised that local farmers were shooting geese heading towards his park, he paid them compensation, an idea at least a century ahead of its time. On the scientific side, his interest in the lives of animals and plants was as strong in his last years as in his earliest, and every experiment, however trivial, was written up in his journal.

Waterton's eccentricities grew daily. He would crawl under the table and bite his guests' ankles at dinner, or hop along the topmost wall of his grotto – a considerable

height – on one leg with the other hanging over the chasm; he made himself a pair of wings and began to consider the possibilities of flying from the roof of a barn.

One of the most delightful descriptions of Waterton comes from his own *Essays on Natural History*. He had gone to London to see the first living orang-utan brought to this country and asked if he might enter its cage. No doubt the assembled onlookers thought he would be torn limb from limb, but what actually happened was very different and is typical of Waterton's extraordinary sensitivity and feeling for animals:

'As I approached the orang-utan he met me about half-way and we soon entered into an examination of each other's persons. Nothing struck me more forcibly than the uncommon softness of the inside of his hands. Those of a delicate lady could not have shown a finer texture. He took hold of my wrist and fingered the blue veins therein contained; while I myself was lost in admiration at the protuberance of his enormous mouth. He most obligingly let me open it and thus I had the opportunity of examining his two fine rows of teeth. We then placed our hands round each other's necks and we kept them there awhile...it were loss of time in me were I to pen down an account of the many gambols which took place betwixt us.'

A female gorilla that had died was sent to Waterton and was turned by him into a superb preserved specimen but, up to his old tricks again, he sewed a pair of donkey's ears onto its head and called it Martin Luther. Other jokes abounded in and around the park: two big trees that had twisted together as they grew were known as 'Church and State', and a collection of toads, lizards, reptiles and scorpions preserved together under a glass dome were known as 'England's Reformation in its Infancy'. In his last years Waterton grew fearful for the future of Walton Hall and his two sisters-in-law who were entirely dependent on him, and with whom he had shared his life for nearly half a century. His biggest problem was that his son Edmund disliked almost everything he had grown up around.

After an apparently minor fall in the park in May 1865 when he was eighty-three, he quickly declined; three days later he was dead. But as his friend Norman Moore (later president of the Royal College of Physicians) said: 'He died just as the rooks were beginning to caw and the swallows to chirp. He died as he always said he would, sitting up and conscious to the last'. He was buried between two massive oak trees at the edge of his beloved lake, and it is said that a flock of birds followed the cortège as his funeral barge moved slowly across the water.

Today the grave is still there, but the oak trees and almost all the other old trees in the park have gone. The house, though much changed and modernised, is recognisably the same and in one or two odd corners are a few of the nesting boxes Waterton fashioned so long ago. The saddest part of the story is that Waterton's premonition that his son would destroy all his good work proved true: within months of his death all the birds had been shot off the lake and the trees sold and felled, and only a few years later Edmund had disposed of the house to raise money to pay his debts. Within a decade Edmund, too, was dead, and the Waterton connection with Walton Hall came to an end for ever.

QUEEN OF THE EAST

Lady Hester Stanhope

Born in 1776, Lady Hester Stanhope spent much of her childhood hoping that it would rain so she would be able to walk about on stilts to avoid the mud. As a young woman she tried to row to France, and was once punished by being made to look after a herd of turkeys. In 1810 she heard an inmate at Bedlam declare that she would become Queen of the East, and therefore set off for Jerusalem. Here the local ruler gave her a house where she simply sat and waited to be crowned queen. Over the long years of waiting that followed she adopted ever more enthusiastically the ways of the east, wearing the local dress and learning to speak Arabic fluently. To visitors she explained this passion for the Middle East by saying she couldn't bear the English because they had flat feet.

By 1840, however, she had run out of money, having spent it all turning a derelict convent into a sumptuous palace. With her fortune spent she simply bricked up all the doors and windows and departed; a few months later she was dead. In her will she asked that she be buried at midnight accompanied by the skull of one of her long-dead lovers with a candle burning in it.

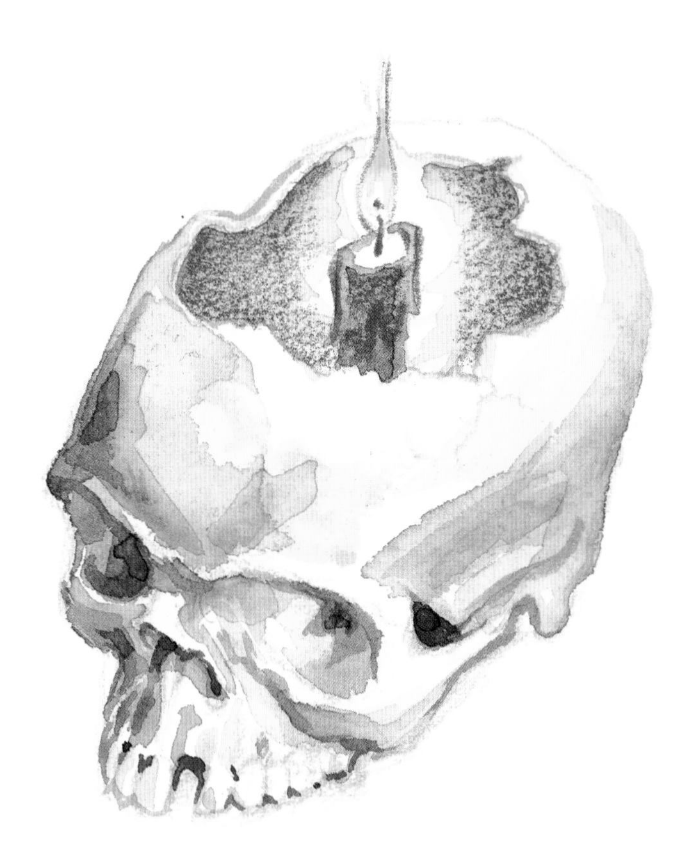

THE GNOME FANCIER

Ann Atkin

West Putford, Devon

Ann Atkin lives in a remote village in north Devon, but pilgrims and visitors from all over Britain and the rest of the world regularly visit her to meet her extraordinary collection of gnomes. Now in her late fifties, and originally from Sussex, Ann has been collecting gnomes for years; she also takes in unhappy and injured ones, as well as those surplus to people's requirements.

Ann and her husband Ron – both professional artists – set up their gnome reserve in West Putford near Bradworthy, north Devon nearly twenty years ago, and such is the fame of the place that it now attracts more than 30,000 visitors a year. The Putford gnomes have been filmed by television crews from all over the world – the Japanese are particularly keen – and they have recently been included in a prestigious guide to the gardens of Great Britain. But this increasing fame has not gone to the gnomes' heads, as Ann explains: 'Well, the mini-men are delighted by all the attention, it is true, but they take it all in their stride.'

There are over 1,000 gnomes in the 4-acre garden; some can be found at work by ponds and under trees – 'They don't all like to be idle,' says Ann – and they vary greatly in size, from about one inch to over three feet high.

'We did get worried a few years ago that no pixies had been given a place in the garden,' says Ann. 'There was a shriek of protest from the pixie fraternity, but the situation has been rectified and now we have lots of lovely pixies. We let visitors have one each when they come, to remind them of their visit – they are like symbols of joy. We make dentist pixies, bus driver pixies, doctor pixies, housewife pixies and so on. Whatever you are you get a pixie to match. The pixies can be found in the half of the garden that is mostly flowers and herbs – we have a total of more than two hundred plant species in the garden – and the gnomes are mostly to be found in our 2½ acres of lovely beech trees. They pop up everywhere!'

The Gnome Reserve and Wildflower Garden, to give it its full title, is looked after by Ann, Ron and their son Richard who is also the chief gnome- and pixie-maker.

'The whole idea about this place is that it is completely serious and yet at the same time completely humorous,' says Ann. 'You either like gnomes or you don't, but lots of people who claim they don't like them or dismiss out of hand the whole idea of a gnome sanctuary are completely converted when they visit us.

'We don't make any hard-and-fast rules for visitors, but we don't like to embarrass or frighten our little men so we do ask everyone to put on a little pointy gnome hat when they arrive. It avoids embarrassment all round and they do look rather nice.'

Ann is a great believer in the spiritual value of her gnomes, and she argues passionately for them as a means to promote peace and bring people together.

'We find that getting all our visitors to wear a gnome hat is a real leveller. Little identical hats can make three generations of the same family feel at one, whatever the age differences. They are so democratic and will help break down all sorts of barriers and defence systems. People come to see us laughing and many leave the same way. Everyone feels they share in the laughter. From every point of view it is such a healthy thing to turn people into gnomes, even if it is only for a day.'

Ann's gnome garden was recently entered for the Turner Art Prize, one of the most valuable and prestigious awards in the country, which has previously been won by the eccentric Damien Hirst for sawing a cow in half. Ann's garden didn't win, but, undaunted, she now organises the annual International Gnome Day at which visitors get to meet gnomes young and old.

Ann's very special card school!

A CAT IN A COAT

Marmalade Emma and Teddy Grimes

Marmalade Emma and Teddy Grimes were two tramps who wandered the countryside around Colchester in the years before the Great War. Teddy wore enormous gold ear-rings and had a long, drooping moustache. He always wore one black boot and one brown, and three heavy overcoats. Emma wore a huge, flowery Victorian dress and a thick tweed jacket in which her cat lived. From a thick rope tied round her waist hung numerous heavy pots and pans. The pair always slept in the open and gave all the best bits of food they were able to scavenge to their cat.

THE SUSSEX PYRAMID BUILDER

Jack Fuller

Mad Jack Fuller of Brightling in Sussex was born in 1757 and spent much of his life building pyramids and towers. In the 1820s he built a 35ft high conical tower called the Sugar Loaf, after betting a London friend that he could see the spire of the church in the village of Dallington some miles from his estate. When he got home he discovered that he couldn't, so he had the cone-shaped tower built in a position that made it just visible, in roughly the position where he'd expected to see the church spire. This was the beginning of a building spree that was to last Fuller the rest of his life.

When Wellington won the Battle of Waterloo, Fuller was so pleased that he employed dozens of local workmen to build a 65ft high memorial tower on top of the highest peak in East Sussex, where it stands to this day. Then he built a 35ft tower on his estate, for reasons known only to himself, together with an enormous classical temple.

When he died in 1834 he had already built his final resting place: a 25ft high stone pyramid in the local churchyard, and here he was buried – sitting bolt upright in a chair with a bottle of wine beside him.

Horatio William Bottomley

THE WORLD'S GREATEST SWINDLER

Horatio William Bottomley

Horatio William Bottomley was a Member of Parliament, a newspaper publisher, journalist and orator, and probably the greatest and most eccentric swindler of all time. He cheated thousands of individuals, institutions, the City and even the government of which he was a member.

Born in Hackney in lowly circumstances early in the nineteenth century, he spent his childhood in an orphanage. He left school at fourteen and became a solicitor's clerk, which gave him the grounding he was later to use to achieve wealth and power.

He bought a small ailing newspaper and a couple of small printing firms, and began to make money; but in spite of the real wealth of the company he could not resist milking it dry. He spent millions on countless schemes of extravagance – horses, travel, country houses and flats in various towns. The company eventually crashed and he ended up in the High Court where he spent much of the trial correcting the judge on points of law, tied the prosecution up in knots, and convinced jury, public and judge that he was a victimised underdog. He escaped with a warning.

He continued on his triumphant way, always insisting on kippers and champagne for breakfast and keeping a string of mistresses in London and the provinces. Never bothering to learn about horses he nonetheless bought and sold and raced them with complete and reckless abandon.

In ten years he spent an estimated £23 million of other people's money, and his success was crowned when, in 1905, he was elected Liberal member of parliament for Hackney. As part of his election campaign he saddled all his racehorses and sent them riderless down Hackney High Street with 'Vote for my owner' emblazoned on their saddles. He ran a sweep through one of his papers on the 1914 Derby, and it was won by a 'little old lady' living near Toulouse; a suspicious journalist discovered that the 'little old lady' was actually Bottomley himself.

Finally he cheated an associate who told all to the courts. He was tried in 1922 and produced another brilliant speech, at the end of which he declared that it would be the most appalling miscarriage of justice if they found him guilty. But it was not enough and he was sentenced to seven years' penal servitude. While sewing mailbags a visitor saw him at work and said, 'Sewing, I see'.

'No, reaping,' he replied. He was released, and died penniless in 1933.

HOW TO GET AHEAD

Simeon Ellerton

Reputedly over a hundred years old when he died in 1799, Simeon Ellerton built a house in his native Durham by collecting stones and carrying them home in a bag on his head. He had been employed as a message carrier for decades, and in the course of his business he found many stones that suited him perfectly; these he brought home.

At last his cottage was finished, but having spent so many years carrying heavy weights on his head he found he could not do without them. Even in retirement he would walk about the town or sit in his garden with a bag of stones on his head.

THE FABULOUS FOOTSLOGGER

Foster Powell

Born at Horseforth near Leeds in 1734, Foster Powell came to London in 1762 to study law. Two years later he began the extraordinary series of walking feats that were to make him famous throughout Britain. He first bet that he could walk 50 miles in 7 hours – and he did it. In 1773, again for a bet, he walked from London to York and back (a distance of over 400 miles) in 5 days and 18 hours. In 1778, by now famous and attracting large crowds to the start of each of his long walks, he ran 2 miles in 10 minutes, an astonishing feat by the standards of the day; in 1786 he walked 100 miles in 24 hours. Numerous other journeys spread his pedestrian fame far and wide. He only ever made any money when, on one trip, he took the wrong turn and failed to reach his goal in the allotted time; the crowd felt sorry for him so they collected over £40. But he said he never really did it for the money; it was for the 'sheer pleasure of perambulation' – and besides, it was easy for him as he never needed more than 5 hours rest in any 24. He died in 1793.

THE MAN IN THE IRON WIG

Edward Montague Wortley

Edward Montague Wortley, who died in 1790, learned Arabic as a young man, grew a huge beard and always wore robes and a turban. He was elected to the Royal Society after inventing an iron wig. He married, bigamously, his washerwoman, a Miss Dormer whom eventually he left to live with a Nubian girl. Reports reached London of his travels around Europe and the Far East because his iron wig, which he wore every day however hot the weather, was so easy to spot.

TRAVELS WITH MY MONKEY

Philip Thicknesse

Born in 1719 in Northampton, Philip Thicknesse was sent to school at Westminster where he earned money by allowing other boys to beat him for so much per stroke. At the age of sixteen he was sent to America 'to retrieve the family fortune'. However, on the other side of the Atlantic he found the Indians far more congenial than the Europeans, and spent so much time with them that he learned at least one of their languages. He published numerous articles attacking the way they were treated by the European settlers, an attitude which was considered highly eccentric at the time. He returned to England in 1737, but went straight off to Jamaica where he spent much of his time defending the slaves against ill-treatment by their owners.

Captain Thicknesse making his Grand Tour with his wife and three children, their pet spaniel, Callee the horse and Jocko the monkey (riding postilion). There is also a parakeet, nestling out of sight, in Mrs Thicknesse's bosom

Thicknesse spent a great deal of his life quarrelling and suing the people who criticised him. His most serious offence was to attack a judge who had found against him, after which he had to leave the country to escape imprisonment. He sailed for France, bought a carriage in Calais and set off in it for Spain with his wife – he was married three times – two daughters, a guitar and viola, a spaniel, a parakeet and a monkey dressed in full livery which rode the carriage horse like a postilion.They meandered down through France and were only stopped by the border guards because they were suspicious about the nationality of the horse! Whenever they met a circus monkey or a circus bear on the road, Thicknesse would leap down from the carriage and introduce *his* monkey.

The family spent some time living in the monastery at Montserrat where the monks apparently found Thicknesse hugely entertaining. By this time he was suffering badly from gallstones, and he tried to cure them by riding his horse vigorously or by driving his carriage over rough roads; he thought that gallstones were a problem only because they had rough edges and that violent movement would knock off the rough edges and thus effect a cure.

When he thought the danger of prosecution had passed, Thicknesse returned with his family to England in 1776 to a house in Bath; here he wrote a book about his life which became a bestseller. He died in 1792 aged seventy-three.

Mystics and Military Men

Colonel A.D. Wintle, surely the most endearingly batty military man who ever lived, once exclaimed: 'Thank God I wasn't born a flea, a monkey or a Frenchman.' The ministry of God has always produced its fair share of delightful characters, too: a former Bishop of Derry, who enjoyed nothing more than organising games of leapfrog with his fellow clerics, and Lord Rokeby, who believed so ardently in the spiritual nature of water that he spent most of his life in the bath!

THE MILITARY MAN

Bill Curtis

Denbigh, North Wales

Bill Curtis comes from a long line of gunpowder makers. He also comes from a long line of military men whose careers were distinguished in various centuries and at various places across the globe. His great-great-great-grandfather, Sir William Curtis, was Lord Mayor of London: Sir William and his son started the gunpowder company of Curtis's and Harvey; another naval ancestor was president of the court martial that tried Captain Bligh for losing the *Bounty*.

A tall, slim, slightly stooping man with enormous charm, an aristocratic demeanour and a thin moustache, Bill has all the darting intensity of a heron.

Endlessly fascinated by his own family history which is well documented, Bill, now in his sixties, was commissioned into the British Army and served in the Far East and Australia before settling down to a successful business career. But from his earliest days he harboured a love for and fascination with guns. If that makes him sound like a sort of Rambo maniac nothing could be further from the truth, for Bill is an expert on academic militaria: guns made this century hold absolutely no interest for him, and his lifelong obsessions are, among other matters, rifles and muskets made for military purposes by the Royal Small Arms Manufactory at Enfield, particularly the group of muzzleloading rifles in .577 calibre broadly classified as Enfields and made between 1853 and 1864.

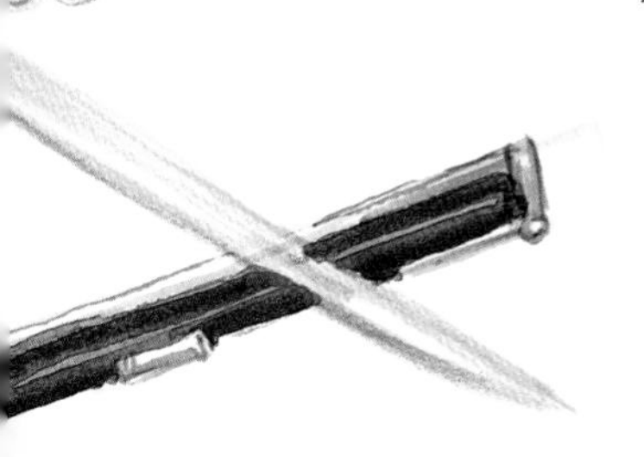

Bill is probably best known for his detailed studies of the literature of shooting during the whole of the eighteenth and nineteenth centuries. To the uninitiated it may seem remarkable that such a relatively narrow subject should provide Bill with a lifetime's study, but to be master of his subject is all the justification Bill needs for hours spent toiling over obscure gunmakers' records, long-vanished firing mechanisms, obsolete muskets and the ammunition they once fired. Nor were these guns better built or more accurate than their modern counterparts: in the vast majority of cases they were difficult to use, cumbersome, slow and inaccurate; but, as Bill would be the first to argue, that is to look at the subject without an historical imagination, because, so far as the early gunmakers, sportsmen and soldiers were concerned, the technology of the time was brilliant within its limitations.

So fascinated is Bill by his subject that he has even set up his own publishing company to re-issue some of the rarest of early shooting books. Among the titles he has so far published the enthusiast will find *Observations (Theoretical and Practical) on Muskets, Rifles and Projectiles Together with a Treatise on the Elastic concave Wadding*, as well as *A Treatise on Air Guns and Other Air Weapons, for shooting with Ball Shot and Harpoons*. There are plenty of people interested in the history of guns, of course, but their interests are broader, more mainstream. Bill Curtis has no desire to be part of the mainstream, however, and if no one else at all had an interest in his subject he would still pursue it as though his life depended on it. He admits himself that whenever, in the early 1950s, he expressed an interest in muzzleloaders he was considered a complete crank. But it is entirely due to his efforts and those of a few others that, forty years later, muzzleloaders are a fully integrated part of the shooting ranges.

'We have moved on considerably from a situation where muzzleloaders were actively discouraged in the 1950s,' says Bill. 'What is more, I can say that the "Old and the Bold" of the 1950s National Rifle Association Council would never have thought it possible that this could have come about.' That it did is due in large part to the efforts of people like Bill.

Bill grew up in rural Sussex where during the war guns became, quietly and unobtrusively, part of his life: 'No one worried about guns in those days,' he says with a hint of sadness and nostalgia in his voice. 'Not the way they do now, anyway. In our village for example there was a Nissen hut at the end of the lane which was absolutely stuffed with guns and ammo and there wasn't even a lock on the door!'

When he left school in 1948 he went to Australia and here, too, guns were seen as an everyday tool. He recalls walking miles along open roads across the military ranges and coming across unlocked huts filled with guns and ammunition, 'and this was the big stuff,' he says with a smile. But the attitude to guns used for sport was very different too: 'It's hard to imagine how different things were in the 1950s. I used to take a shotgun without a case or a cover on the bus or train and no one thought anything of it. Can you imagine doing that now!'

Bill's big, rambling, Victorian house reveals numerous prints and pictures of illustrious ancestors; an early engraving of his great-great-great-grandfather as Lord Mayor of London is the most notable, along with a framed Peninsular War medal awarded to the great early nineteenth-century sportsman Colonel Peter Hawker. Between digressions into the world of gun lore and occasional forays into powder mills and shot towers, Bill explains the history of his huge collection of guns and accessories; but first he recounts the exploits of one or two of his famous ancestors:

'Sir William was a friend of the Prince Regent and went with him to France and Scotland in 1821. Apart from having friends in high places Sir William also had the biggest yacht in the Royal Yacht Squadron. He was hugely rich, and he, a nephew and his son – my great-great-grandfather – founded Curtis's and Harvey, the gunpowder makers. The family ran the firm from about 1820 until just after the Great War. They were the biggest powder-makers in the world and I suppose it was in some measure that fact that inspired my early interest in the subject of guns and gunpowder. Curtis's and Harvey merged with other makers to become, in the 1920s, Nobel and eventually ICI.

'My father and grandfather fought in World War I, and my great-grandfather was at the siege of Sebastopol; he commanded the heavy mortars of the "Right Attack". My grandfather was mentioned in despatches, so I suppose you could say that the family has something of a military history!' Bill hurtles through the history of the family, and then through his own history which also has a military connection:

'I had a short service commission in the Royal Artillery in 1954, and before that in the Artillery Militia in Australia which was most interesting; in Britain we were always worried about shortages of things and generally muddled along, whereas in Australia it was all so utterly different. In 1955 I was at Bisley commanding a bunch of soldiers from Woolwich. My interest in muzzle-loaders, however, preceded my army career and I'd really got started I suppose in 1950.'

The muzzleloader was the usual form of gun available before the widespread introduction of the breechloader, which is the basis of all modern guns. To load a muzzleloader, a charge of gunpowder was measured and poured down the barrel of the gun (hence the gun was loaded from the muzzle). This was followed by a piece of wadding, a sort of felt or paper pad to keep the shot in position and keep everything tight in the barrel. Next the shot was measured and poured down the barrel; then more wadding, and finally it was all rammed home with a ramrod, a long thin rod of wood or steel that fitted below and parallel to the barrel when not in use. All this may sound rather laborious, but when Bill demonstrates the military procedure for loading – and he is an expert who looks as if he's spent his life doing it – you can see how a trained soldier in Wellington's army was able to fire the regulation four shots a minute.

'The King of Prussia insisted on six shots a minute,' says Bill, while standing to attention and running through the loading procedure at lightning speed. Of course there were accessories that made loading easier, for example flasks that allowed the right amount of powder to be dispensed, shot measurers and so on; but as Bill explains with passionate enthusiasm, it was because of the excellent technique, skill and training of the individual soldiers that troops produced such extraordinarily rapid shooting with what appears by modern standards woefully inadequate equipment. 'Although,' says Bill, 'it's worth remembering that the military musket used a kind of cartridge which was a simple tube of paper containing both powder and ball.

'But it's the gunpowder that's really interesting,' he continues, just when we are getting deeply involved in the details of fractional design differences between one muzzleloading Enfield and the next. 'I've made my own gunpowder a few times just out of interest, but it is difficult to make it as well as the professionals. It's still manufactured in many countries, though sadly no longer in the UK. When I went to Australia in 1948 the things you could still buy in the gun and gunpowder line were quite extraordinary. Do you know, they still had Curtis's and Harvey gunpowder in its pre-war tins, and these weren't being sold as antiques or curiosities, they were simply being sold to shooting men for everyday use! Extraordinary! The shops even sold nineteenth-century caps – they still had them in stock, just lying around after more than fifty years! I think it was because they hadn't had the disruption of war as we'd had in England.'

Bill reckons he was the only muzzleloading shooter alive in Victoria, Australia during the 1950s; but from tiny beginnings the sport of muzzleloading has grown hugely. In the early 1970s just six countries worldwide met each year to discuss muzzleloaders and to compete with them; now some twenty-six countries meet every year, and this resurgence of interest has a lot to do with people such as Bill who were so anxious to keep the ancient traditions alive long before they were even remotely fashionable. As he says, 'Muzzleloading never quite died out completely, but it came pretty close, and it was really only puntgunners and a few wildfowlers in remote areas of Britain who kept the old guns and techniques going.'

In 1952 the Muzzleloaders' Association of Great Britain spearheaded an attempt to keep the old traditions alive. 'I joined in 1956,' says Bill proudly, 'but there were still only a few of us and information was sometimes hard to come by. For twenty-five years I was variously treasurer, editor and chairman, but there are four broad categories of member: the collector who may or may not shoot (pure collectors tend not to join); the collector who likes shooting; those who collect and fire original guns; and those who collect and fire modern replicas.'

As far as Bill is concerned any and every gun in which he is likely to take an interest must be authentic. 'I do have a replica and it's a good one, but it's not as good as the real thing. There's something almost indefinably marvellous about old guns, the way they were put together, and the subject is so complex and endlessly fascinating.' Bill leaps up at this point and opens a massive mahogany corner cupboard packed full of guns which, to the untrained eye, look virtually identical. One by one he takes them out and lays them lovingly on the floor. Each illustrates a phase in the development of his beloved Enfield. He has no interest in the later Lee Enfields: for Bill, a gun worth collecting and firing has to be an Enfield rifle, 'or perhaps an early Whitworth'.

Patient with those whose ignorance of guns must sometimes astound him, Bill explains the difference between a rifle and a musket: 'It's very simple – well, in some senses it's simple, if one is prepared to simplify it. A musket has a smooth barrel, whereas a rifle has rifling – that is, spiral grooves cut along the inside of the barrel to make the bullet spin as it leaves the gun and thereby improve accuracy.' And Bill knows his Enfields down to the degree of rifling that the various models were given, the changes that occurred in length of stock, type of trigger and style of decoration.

But what is the appeal of these ancient weapons to the man who doesn't just want to collect and admire them? Why do people like Bill have to imitate and reproduce precisely a long-lost gunnery technique? 'We enjoy the ballistics, the look of the guns, the historical re-creation it entails and the fact that the early gunmakers and practitioners of those days produced such marvellous results without the aid of modern technology; and, most important of all, we want to make these guns shoot as well as when they were new.'

Bill's enthusiasm is all the more extraordinary because the gunpowder his guns use is traditional black powder, which is notoriously difficult to use, varying in its firing qualities and producing huge volumes of smoke once the gun has been fired. This is why films that re-create early battles always show enormous confusion, largely caused by the dense clouds of light grey impenetrable gunsmoke.

'Black powder is a delight to use, but it is dirty, I agree,' says Bill. 'Modern smokeless powder is precisely that – smokeless, but that's why it has so little interest. Frankly, it's boring stuff. Black powder produces a slow, steady push up the barrel, not the instant nasty crack of modern cordite, and the steady push is followed by a slow, heavy recoil. Trajectories are much higher with black powder, too, so distance judging is more difficult. Modern guns shoot flat at 300 yards, whereas an old muzzleloader – I am thinking of a particular flintlock target rifle now – might have a trajectory like a rainbow; but if you know what you're doing it's much more satisfactory to shoot well with such a gun.'

As well as being a member of the Muzzleloaders Association, Bill is a key figure in three even more obscure organisations: the Historical Breechloaders Association, the Crimean

War Research Society and the Gunpowder Mills Study Group. Of this last, Bill says: 'We have forty members and we are all very interested indeed in this aspect of the history of guns and gunpowder.' He shoots game and clay pigeons with his guns, and in his current role as vice-president of MLAGB keeps an eye on changes in legislation that may make life more difficult for muzzleloaders: 'We've got the local constabularies tamed now!' he says with evident relish. 'People used to think we were all a bit daft, but it's a serious sport. Forty years ago the rifle clubs would try to get the muzzleloaders thrown off the ranges, but now we are recognised as serious enthusiasts.'

Bill's eyes light up when he begins to discuss his beloved guns; even the construction of the barrels of a gun produces a torrent of enthusiasm: 'Modern guns are bored from solid lumps of steel – indeed, deep hole boring is an art in itself and deserves separate study – but early guns were made either by wrapping flat metal around a mandrel and then joining it up with a longitudinal seam, or by twisting a strip of metal along the mandrel producing what are known as twist or damascus barrels. These can be made in such a way that the barrel has a lovely, almost arabesque pattern in it, and different customers might ask for different twists in order to get the appearance they desired. However out of date they may seem, damascus barrels still have advantages over their modern steel counterparts: if a barrel bursts, for example, the iron of the damascus tends to buckle whereas the steel of a modern barrel will explode, causing the shooter more injury. Iron wasn't nearly so brittle.'

Having explained that the eighteenth-century infantryman could get off four shots a minute with his land service musket – indeed, that is what he was trained to achieve as a minimum – Bill moves on to the vast and intricate subject of the systems for igniting the powder, systems such as the flintlock or the percussion cap lock.

'I have rather unorthodox views on ignition,' he says mysteriously, 'because although it is important I don't think it is as important as the barrel. The 1715 musket with its flintlock has precisely the same barrel as the 1842 percussion musket; even the calibre or bore is the same, .75 or ¾in. The 1715 musket would have been made by different contractors on behalf of the Board of Ordnance, again a complete subject in itself. The government went to a barrel maker for the barrels, to Wolverhampton or somehere like it for the locks – the Midlands was always a great centre of gunmaking – and then they went to Birmingham or London to have the different bits assembled into the finished gun. By 1859 things were changing, and although private contractors were still active, the Enfield factory was making all the parts *and* assembling them; it used to take two and a half minutes to take the parts and make a gun from them. I can strip an Enfield into its sixty-two parts, drop them in a bag, rattle them about and then tell you exactly which bit is which.'

Bill can explain the manufacture of Enfields intimately, even though the factory closed before he was born. He is also an authority on general military history, and takes great delight in explaining how, in just forty years, the army progressed from using ancient smooth-bore muskets to twentieth-century hi-tech 303s:

'The artillery had always been rather complacent in war because they were at the back of the action and could fire their case-shot or round shot over at the enemy without the risk of being fired back at. Then, suddenly, with the introduction of rifles they found they were being fired back at, and they didn't like it at all! That was really where the idea of trenches started – people didn't like being shot at from a distance by an accurate weapon such as a rifle so they dug holes to hide in! But remember the artillery men and the engineers were the only trained soldiers in the British army; those boys were scientists, and got their commissions by exam. Compared to them, the infantry officers were mere playboys.'

All at once Bill returns to the subject of locks and means of ignition, obviously a subject near to his heart because he must know nearly all there *is* to know about everything from the earliest matchlocks (a burning taper pushed down on to the powder by the action of the trigger) to the first rudimentary percussion gun systems. 'I've also engaged in a detailed study of the Whitworth hexagonal bored rifle,' he says, darkly. 'It was the first long-range rifle. Whitworth is important because Joseph Whitworth was the first to establish the relationship between calibre, length of bullet and the spiral of the rifling and the velocity of the gun.'

Then we are back to the Enfield, which Bill describes with unqualified affection.

'People don't realise that although the musket was a muzzleloader, the men used a primitive cartridge with it. They would carry the bullet, the ball, wadding and powder in position in a tube of paper ready to be popped down the barrel, and they would have a quantity of these ready made up in a pouch. The idea was that they pulled out a paper tube, tore the end off with their teeth, and tipped a bit of powder into the pan on the lock (the bit that ignites the main charge); then they'd pour the rest of the powder down the barrel and pop the ball, still wrapped in its paper, down afterwards. Skirmishers who were employed to creep about used guns with rifled barrels, but they still had round ball to fire rather than modern bullets. In these rifles the round ball would be forced into the gun using a mallet – you needed a tight fit so the ball could grip the rifling and gain its spinning motion. But different nationalities reacted differently to the introduction of rifles; the Germans loved them, the French hated them.'

Among Bill's beloved Enfields are some extremely rare models; he owns one which was made specifically for use by sergeants, and it is so rare that when the Royal Armouries at the Tower of London needed an example they had to come to Bill. But Enfields were endlessly modified, and although Bill has many examples of guns with these modifications, to the untrained eye there is absolutely no discernible difference between any of them.

Bill firmly believes that guns are an important part of social history. One particular story he is fond of telling relates how, after the Indian Mutiny, native troops were only ever given guns with crude sights and smooth bores: in other words, vastly inferior weapons, because this would reduce the danger if ever they mutinied again. With a vast collection of books on guns and shooting – and this includes a copy of all eleven editions of Colonel Hawker's *Instructions to Young Sportsmen* – Bill is an expert on oval and octagonal bores, patchlocks, matchlocks, flintlocks, Augustine Console locks and much besides. He also owns one or two extraordinarily beautiful guns by some of the greatest of all sporting gunmakers, men like Purdey and Manton. He owns a powder carrier's lid dredged up from a ship that sank in the Solent in 1758, and he has a Purdey with the only surviving trade label from the short period when the company was based at No 315 Oxford Street. He has hundreds of shooting accessories ranging from strange powder flasks to even stranger sighting devices, ancient cartridges and tiny eighteenth-century ladies' pistols complete with their original bullets. Truly Bill's interest can be called an all-consuming passion.

SOOTHSAYER

Swein Macdonald

Ardgay, Ross-shire

High on a hill above the Cromarty Firth some fifty miles north of Inverness lives Swein Macdonald, a big man with a snowy white beard; his grandfather built the present family house, and his family has lived on this remote croft for centuries. His name, Swein, has been handed down through the male line of the family since it was given, probably in the ninth or tenth century, by a distant ancestor who came over with a Viking raiding party and then married a local woman.

Above Swein's head in the old sitting-room hangs an ancient sword, used by one of his ancestors at Culloden; like most Highland Scots, Swein sees the past as ever present, which is hardly surprising in a land where the bitterness caused by the clearances of whole communities in Victorian times is still keenly felt. But if most Highlanders have a great sense of the past, few have such a keen sense of the future as Swein for he is a visionary, a soothsayer, for whom the future is sometimes as clear as the past. He doesn't examine your hand or the bumps on your head in order to predict your future, he just knows. But as he himself is the first to admit, he can't always do it, and his glimpses into the future of others come unbidden. But how did this remarkable ability develop?

'Well,' he explains, 'it didn't really *develop* at all, I think it's just in the family. My grandfather certainly had the gift – he always knew when someone was going to die – and I believe one of my sons will inherit it.' Like his grandfather, Swein sometimes sees both good and bad, but he is a gentle, discreet man who knows when it is best to keep silent.

'If something bad is on the horizon I usually say nothing. I'll give you an example. A woman came to me with her mother and I wouldn't tell her anything. A week later the daughter telephoned and said she understood why I had said nothing: her mother had just died, and it is true that when I had first seen her, the mother appeared to be wearing a shroud. That told me everything.'

Away from his soothsaying, Swein is a practical farmer with a thousand acres of sheep grazing and woodland to look after. He used to farm long-horned Highland cattle – 'they're glorious beasts,' he says – but like most farmers, he found that keeping such an old-fashioned breed just didn't make economic sense. These days he keeps only sheep, but they certainly provide more than enough work for a man who also receives dozens of telephone calls and letters from all over the world asking for his help and advice.

'I do a lot of work for the police, and I've appeared on television. You see, I don't need tea leaves or palmistry or anything. I only need to hear or see the person concerned; so I can often predict things just from a telephone call, or I can tell from a letter.

'The police often come to me when someone has gone missing, and I've helped with several cases like that. I'll give you an example. A woman went missing several years

ago up at Brora. She was a crofter's wife, and although she was very well known locally the police had no luck finding her; but I told them she would be found in a certain loch on a certain day, and that she would be found by a man with two sheepdogs. They searched the loch from end to end and told me that if she'd been there they'd have found her – but of course they were looking too soon. I knew it would be a week or so later. I don't think anyone believed me, until she was found in precisely the way I'd described.'

Another of Swein's notable successes was the case of the London woman whose son had gone missing. She rang Swein asking for help and he promised he would do what he could. At about the same time an Inverness man went missing, and shortly afterwards a body was found in a loch; it was identified by the Inverness man's father, but Swein was convinced that this was a case of mistaken identity – the body, he insisted, was *not* that of the man from Inverness: 'I was quite sure they had got the wrong man. In spite of the father's positive identification I knew the young man in the loch was the London woman's son. Then on the day the Inverness boy was supposed to be buried, he walked into his home in Inverness. It was just as I'd said, and the young man in the loch was indeed the London woman's son.'

Like most of Swein's insights these came in the form of pictures, and they have come to him in one form or another almost for as long as he can remember. 'I was about three or four when it first happened. I was down in the field with my mother shifting stones when suddenly in my head I saw grandfather in bed, unwell and with a man in black leaning over him. A few minutes later my mother asked me to take something to my grandfather who was actually working in a field nearer the house. I said I wouldn't go because I was frightened. I knew he was ill. My mother insisted he was perfectly healthy. About fifteen minutes later we were called up to the house because grandfather had just had an accident and broken three ribs. The doctor, who always dressed in black, had been called.'

Swein was born in Elgin – 'I should have been born in this house, but my mother wanted a day out!' – sixty-five years ago. At that time the Highlands still seemed very remote indeed, with open fires in every house, no television, wet and dry radios – 'terrible interference,' says Swein with a laugh – and roads unmade until well into the 1950s. But this very remoteness and the sense of continuity in families such as Swein's – families able to trace their ancestors back centuries – no doubt contributed to the rich, imaginative life that lies at the heart of his remarkable abilities.

The Highlands are far more accessible today, but their special atmosphere may explain why, although he worked in Africa and in other countries for a number of years, Swein always knew that he would eventually return. Physical remoteness doesn't stop the visitors coming, however, and Swein's growing reputation means that they now come in increasing numbers. He has to deal with telephone calls, letters and flying visits from all over the world. One group of Germans even hired a helicopter and landed in his back garden, three businessmen who wanted to know if they ought to go ahead and make a certain investment in property.

'They hadn't been able to make up their minds,' he says with a grin, 'and someone suggested they come to see me to get a final decision. I told them to go ahead, and they never got back to me so I suppose it was all right. On another occasion a Japanese man came to me to ask if he should send his son to school at Gordonstoun; I thought it probably couldn't do any harm! He couldn't even speak English and had to come with an interpreter!'

However, most of the questions that Swein is asked relate to what one might describe as the smaller matters in life: will marriages last, what shall I do with my business, shall I change my job, will my child be successful. But Swein treats them all with the same Highland courtesy and *gravitas*, and if he *can* help, he will.

THE LAST ENGLISHMAN

Colonel Alfred Daniel Wintle

In his autobiography Lieutenant Colonel Alfred Daniel Wintle claimed that he had spent his life fighting against injustice, pomposity and hypocrisy; he was also, throughout his long and active life, wildly and entertainingly eccentric in almost every respect. He was born in 1897 in Russia where his father was employed as a diplomat. In spite of his Russian birth, or perhaps because of it, Wintle got down on his knees every night before he went to bed and thanked God for making him an Englishman: being an Englishman, according to Wintle, was 'the highest responsibility as well as the greatest honour'.

He was besotted by the idea of Englishness and utterly biased against every other nation, and for as long as he could remember had always wanted to be an English soldier; however, his European upbringing meant that he spoke German and French 'at all times of the day' and was steeped in the culture of western and central Europe. Later in life he justified his dislike of other nationalities by saying: 'There are two classes of insular Englishmen; those who think no foreigner is as good as an Englishman through sheer ignorance, and those, like me, who know it through experience.' During his first stay in England, with an aunt in Clapham when he was about ten, he developed the

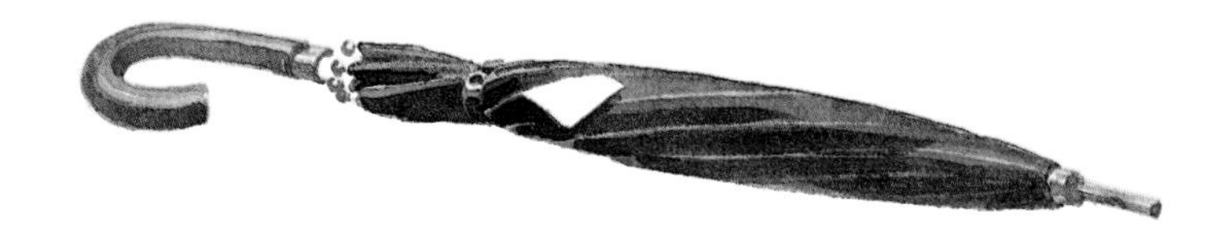

few great loves of his life: horses, cricket, vegetable marrows, country railway stations and umbrellas. The gift of an umbrella when he was twelve made him feel he was 'on the way to becoming a complete English gentleman – it was the apple of my eye'. In fact he was so fond of this umbrella that for many years he slept with it every night and always left a note in it when he rolled it up which said 'This umbrella has been stolen from A.D.Wintle'.

Wintle believed that knowledge of the uses of umbrellas and a proper regard for them was the true mark of a gentleman; umbrellas also lay at the heart of the difference between the Englishman and the Frenchman or German. 'The Frenchman gets up in the morning,' explained Wintle, 'and consults his barometer. If there is to be no rain he leaves his umbrella at home, sallies forth and gets a drenching. The Englishman, by contrast, is too stupid to understand all these barometers and things so he always takes his umbrella with him. But it doesn't end there, for whatever the circumstances no Englishman ever unfurls his umbrella, which means he gets wet.'

Wintle's unconditional love of the English and all things English began before he had even set foot in the country. He was first sent to school in France and early on remembered his feelings of indignation when the teacher announced to the class that Mont Blanc was higher than Snowdon. Wintle reported the matter to his father who told him 'There's nothing clever about having the highest mountain in Europe growing in your country. It's infinitely more important to be English.' Wintle's father was strict, but by all accounts a man of action, and these were qualities his son was to inherit in large measure.

At the age of twelve the young Wintle was sent to school in Germany where he apparently immediately decided that it would be best if he spoke the language with a Rhineland accent. 'We Rhinelanders winced and writhed later on at the sound of Hitler's common Austrian accent,' he recalled, as if a regional accent was one of Hitler's greatest faults. But despite his oft-repeated dislike of Germans as a race, Wintle in fact had many German friends and a great deal of respect for their culture, and for years after the war ended he regularly sent food parcels to these friends. As a boy, however, he had decided against the Germans after watching them compete in a boat race: when the winner reached the finish all the other boats simply gave up and drifted to the side of the river. The young Wintle was horrified: 'I was beginning to see the Boche in a new light,' he said. Years later he wrote a sort of memo about the Germans which clearly derived from that early experience of their attitude to the boat race: 'As soon as they think they may lose this war they will all give up. England can never be beaten by the unsporting Germans.'

It was the same with the French, though Wintle always believed that the problem with French children was that they were never beaten. The solution he proposed was simple: De Gaulle should take a million young Scots girls back to France and make them nannies to a million French children. But with his usual contrariness Wintle, though he claimed to despise the French, was constantly doing little acts of kindness for individual Frenchmen; for example he once left enough money for an elderly Frenchman to have an extra glass of wine every day for ten years.

As soon as World War I started Wintle joined up. On his very first day in the trenches the soldier standing next to him was blown to pieces. Wintle was so terrified that he stood stock still – and then saluted. 'That did the trick,' he said later, 'and within thirty seconds I had again become an Englishman of action.' A few months later he narrowly missed being killed when a shell blew him off his horse. He lost his left eye and most of his left hand, but he was apparently more concerned about the welfare of his horse and was greatly relieved to hear that it had been unharmed. He demanded to be kept on active service in spite of his wounds, but to his fury the authorities insisted on sending him home. One of his first exploits in the hospital to which he was sent was to dress up as a nurse and go to the nurses' ball. He was caught only because matron spotted that he was still wearing his monocle.

With the sight fully restored to his remaining eye he discharged himself a few weeks later; when a senior nurse tried to stop him leaving he told her that if she didn't get out of his way he would take his trousers off in front of her – that did the trick. Back in uniform he decided that the only way to get back to France was to make his uniform look absolutely perfect and then make his own way back. So having spent a night polishing, brushing and cleaning it, that's exactly what he did. In the final weeks of the war he

the war he was awarded the MC, but always said he couldn't really remember why.

When the armistice was signed he noted in his diary: 'I declare private war on Germany.' And from that day on he always said that he knew the Germans were merely lying low, and that the first and second World Wars were parts one and two of the same war; something with which many historians later came to agree. As part of his campaign to convince officialdom that the war really wasn't over at all, he lobbied Whitehall officials continually until they could stand it no more and he was posted to Ireland. Disappointed, he nonetheless enjoyed numerous compensations, such as the chance to ride virtually every day. 'It is impossible to be unhappy on the back of a horse,' he wrote, adding that 'all time out of the saddle is wasted and can never be regained. Dismounted persons have never lived.'

It must have been a great joy to Wintle when in 1921 he was transferred to the cavalry. He was posted to India, but here he immediately fell out with a fellow officer who also wore a monocle. Wintle despised the man because he had his monocle tied to a piece of string – most ungentlemanly. Wintle kept his own monocle in day and night simply by jamming it into his eye socket; even in the thick of battle, it never once fell out.

Like so many eccentrics, Wintle loved practical jokes and irreverence: on one occasion a senior officer wrote him a memo saying that the lavatory in his room was cracked, and asked what he should do about it; Wintle replied by sending the following memo: 'I suggest a milder laxative.'

In 1923 Wintle achieved his ultimate ambition: he was posted to the Tangier horse, the 1st Royal Dragoons. On his first day he paraded the troop under him and asked which men drank beer; only one stepped forward. He was immediately given ten shillings by Wintle and told to go and get a drink; the rest were given a roasting for such unsavoury habits as drinking tea. He then showed his men how to muck out by picking up armfuls of dung without either a fork or spade, and carrying them out of the stables. Throughout the 1920s he trained and disciplined his men, wherever he happened to be, with the sole aim of fighting the Germans, much to the astonishment and annoyance of the rest of the army.

Recovering in hospital during the 1930s after breaking his leg in a fall, Wintle met Boy (Cedric) Mays, who was to become a lifelong friend. Mays was dangerously ill with mastoiditis and diphtheria in a ward just down the corridor from Wintle. He was not expected to live, but Wintle heard of the young soldier's plight and visited him. His first words to Mays were: 'What's all this nonsense about dying? You know it is an offence for a Royal Dragoon to die in bed. And when you get up, get your bloody hair cut!' Astonishingly it worked, and Mays recovered. He later said that after Wintle's order he had been afraid to die.

Throughout these years of waiting for what he always called part two of the war against the Germans, Wintle managed to indulge in some remarkable pranks including endless chair-jumping competitions. He also acquired a dog called Jumbo to which he became deeply attached; from then on he never went anywhere without it, arguing that dogs, like horses, were far cleverer than humans. On leave in England on one occasion he bought an ancient house at Wrotham in Kent; many years later he was to retire there.

By 1938 he was working in military intelligence, but he couldn't remain silent in the face of what he saw as his superiors' incompetence. 'Our slowness during the year we gained at Munich was appalling,' he said, 'and if our leaders had been deliberate traitors they could not have played Germany's game better.' So furious did he become that at the beginning of 1939 he insisted on an interview with the man he held chiefly responsible for Britain's dithering. When he met the official, who was also an army officer, he told him that he regretted he was not rich enough to buy a 500lb bomb; 'I should wheel such a bomb into the inner courtyard of the War Office,' he told him. He just could not believe that there were officials who still insisted there would be no war.

Once the war began, Wintle made strenuous efforts to get involved in active service, even though by this time he was well into middle age. He went to see his MP, and presented himself at medical boards disguising the fact that he'd lost an eye; but it did no good. He even attempted to get to France by impersonating a senior officer and trying to steal an aeroplane from RAF Hendon. When that failed – he was caught almost as the plane began to taxi along the runway – he tried to have himself discharged from the army. But it was too late, and the incident with the plane led to a court martial because Air Commodore Boyle, the man Wintle had tried to impersonate, decided to prosecute. Before the trial date was set, however, Wintle visited Boyle, waved his gun at him, and told him that he ought to be shot for doing so little to further the war effort.

Next morning Wintle was arrested and told he would be taken to the Tower of London. His escort then lost the warrant for the arrest, so having calmed the man down, Wintle went and got another warrant for himself. He always said that he must have been the only British officer ever to have signed his own arrest warrant to the

Colonel Alfred Daniel Wintle (left) and Cedric Mays (Hulton-Getty Picture Collection)

Tower of London, for that indeed was where he was taken. When he first arrived everyone cut him dead, but word quickly spread as to why he was really there and he became the toast of the place. Soon he was feasting on cigars and champagne and the best food money could buy, and he enjoyed the experience enormously: 'If there hadn't been a war I might have enjoyed a life sentence,' he said.

By now the authorities were thoroughly embarrassed by the whole affair and offered Wintle a way out. But to their horror he insisted on a trial, which he thought would be great fun. The charges were: that he had expressed the view that ministers should be shot; that he had feigned blindness in one eye to evade military service; and that he had threatened a superior officer. To the first charge Wintle replied that he wanted to name specific ministers, a proposition which caused the charge to be quickly dropped; to the second he replied that rather than pretending he was blind he had actually pretended that he could see with both eyes when he couldn't; and to the third charge he replied that the man he'd threatened was a civil servant and not by any means his superior officer. He was found guilty of assault and given a severe reprimand.

Back in the saddle, both literally and metaphorically, he was posted to North Africa where he raced around, always on horseback, working for military intelligence. Because of his fluency in French and German he was then sent to work undercover in Nazi-occupied France. In spite of his language skills and the fact that he had taken the precaution of dyeing his hair blond he was eventually caught. Imprisoned in a damp cell in an old fortress he marched up and down every day for months before managing to escape. He was quickly recaptured and immediately went on hunger strike, and then began haranguing his guards – they were French but were working for the Germans – for being slovenly and ill-disciplined. This eventually produced the absurd situation in which Wintle was being let out each day to parade and inspect the men who were supposed to be guarding him! Then came orders that he was to be shot for being a spy. Miraculously, on the eve of his execution, he slipped away and made his way precariously back to England via Spain. Years later he discovered that the commandant of the fort where he had been held had been so inspired by him that with his 280 men he had gone over to the French Resistance the day after Wintle had escaped.

At the end of the war Wintle retired himself from the army by standing for the parliamentary seat of West Norwood, under the slogan 'The last person who went into the House of Commons with good intentions was Guy Fawkes. It's time they had someone else, like me, with explosive ideas.' Needless to say he lost, but he was out of the army. He spent the next few years quietly in the country or visiting friends in London. His greatest love, apart from gardening and sawing logs, was visiting his favourite pubs, such as the Wig and Pen in London's Fleet Street. He was having a drink there on his own one day when a West Indian dustman came in, absolutely exhausted, and asked for a beer. 'We do not serve beer,' he was told, followed by 'Get out!' Wintle leapt up and shouted, 'Ah, my dear fellow. So glad you could make it. I'm so sorry we can't offer beer, how about champagne?' They spent the next hour or so in lively conversation over a bottle of Moët.

If Wintle was always eager to seek out justice for himself, he was no less the champion of those he felt were being unfairly treated: 'I believe the important difference between the English and all foreigners is that the English are always willing to help a lame dog over a stile,' he once said. And in this context, just when he must have thought that quiet retirement lay ahead for him, his last great battle was about to begin.

The story began with his sister, Marjorie. She had looked after a certain Kitty Wells, a wealthy elderly relative of Wintle's, for more than twenty years until her death. It was then discovered that Kitty Wells had left her considerable fortune to a Brighton solicitor, Frederick Nye. The will was hugely complex and Wintle believed that it had been drawn up by Nye – the main beneficiary – deliberately to cheat Kitty Wells, who would not have been able to understand it when she signed it.

At first Wintle simply wrote to Nye to express his concern. Nye didn't reply. Undaunted, Wintle began his campaign against the solicitor. He printed gross libels about Nye in the local papers. Still no response. Wintle then kidnapped Nye and took him to a hotel room, removed his trousers, photographed him wearing a paper dunce's hat, and then turned him out (still trouserless) into the streets of Brighton. This was too much even for a lawyer. Wintle was arrested, but then that was what he had wanted. He was sent to prison for six months and the legal profession, closing ranks to protect a crook because he was one of them, did nothing about the increasingly obvious outrage that Nye had committed.

In and around the village of Wrotham, Wintle became something of a hero. And when he was released from the Scrubs six months later, he again went on the attack. Assisted by Cedric Mays, whom he had brought back to life all those years ago, Wintle took Nye to court. Again the law simply protected one of its own and Wintle lost; he was ordered to pay all the costs and was bankrupted. The legal system, as so often, had triumphed over justice. Wintle, however, remained unperturbed: 'If a cavalry officer falls on his backside,' he said, 'he immediately remounts and goes on again.'

And that's exactly what he did. Even when his application for legal aid was refused – effectively making him a pauper – he merely observed that he might have been made a pauper but at least he was an English pauper. Nye must have been laughing up his sleeve, but he had not reckoned with the last Englishman. With Mays' help, Wintle appealed to the House of Lords, spent three days presenting his own case – and to the astonishment of everyone, he won. The Lords made the point that if *they* found it impossible to understand the deliberately obscure will, it was reasonable to assume that when Kitty Wells was persuaded to sign it, she could not have understood it either. This was the first time a layman had represented himself and won his case in the Lords.

Penniless but victorious, Wintle returned to Wrotham and at least had the satisfaction of seeing Nye stripped of his ill-gotten gains. The whole affair had taken ten years.

During the last years of his life Wintle spent his time happily growing marrows and other vegetables. He had once expressed the wish that he'd like Schubert's Serenade played by the Royal Dragoons at his funeral, and Mays had said he would arrange it. But when Wintle died in 1966, the Dragoons were overseas. Nothing daunted and in a spirit that Wintle himself would have applauded, Mays fortified himself with the greater part of a bottle of whisky, went into the nave of Canterbury Cathedral, stood to attention, and sang the whole thing on his own.

NORMAN SHAW BUILDING
NORTH

GOLDILOCKS THE BARRISTER

Sir Nicholas Hardwick Fairbairn, MP

Member of Parliament for Perth, brilliant advocate, painter and notorious, much-loved clown, Sir Nicholas Fairbairn was the consummate aristocratic eccentric. Born in 1933, his childhood was extremely privileged but troubled, largely because his parents spent most of their time throwing plates and vases at each other.

He studied medicine at Edinburgh, then switched to classics in order that he might ultimately study for the bar. He was a terrific showman, and at one of his very first cases he turned up wearing an extremely tall hat which he removed in court to reveal a mass of dyed bright yellow hair. The effect of his curls was set off by an immaculate wing collar, a brightly coloured waistcoat and a silver watch-chain. Having established himself as a successful criminal and divorce lawyer he founded the Society for the Preservation of Duddingston Village, just outside Edinburgh.

He was an advocate of birth control long before it was fashionable or even respectable, and once incurred enormous criticism for saying during a famine in Africa that rather than send food we should send contraceptives. He entered Parliament in 1974 and became a great fan of Mrs Margaret Thatcher, who rewarded him with the job of Solicitor General for Scotland.

He divorced his first wife in 1979, and later married again when he designed the clothes for both bride and groom himself, choosing Indian dress for both. In fact Fairbairn designed and made all his clothes from the end of the 1980s until his death in February 1995 aged sixty-one. He was described by one MP as looking, typically, like a park keeper.

He listed his recreations in *Who's Who* as making love, ends meet and people laugh.

A LEAPFROGGING BISHOP

Frederick Hervey, Bishop of Derry

Born in 1730, Hervey studied at Westminster and Cambridge. Through the influence of his brother, Lord Bristol, he was then made Bishop of Cloyne, though as he himself admitted he had absolutely no connection with or interest in Ireland. However, he soon started manoeuvring for the bishopric of Derry which was worth more money than Cloyne, again using the influence of his brother, and he was successful. When he heard the news he was playing leapfrog with his fellow clergy in the garden at Cloyne Palace and is reported to have shouted: 'I will jump no more, gentlemen. I have surpassed you all, and jumped from Cloyne to Derry!'

He was thirty-nine, married, and earning a reputation as an eccentric largely because he was sympathetic to the local Catholic population which, under English rule, could own virtually nothing nor hold any office of any worth. His outspokenness on the subject almost led to him being impeached for treason, and Walpole, Charles James Fox and most other English parliamentarians thought him mad, bad and dangerous to know.

He got nowhere with his radical views, however, and developed instead his personality. He built three huge houses, his favourite being the size of Blenheim Palace, perched on a cliff top at Lough Foyle. On the death of his brother in 1778 he became Lord Bristol. His house parties were legendary; he would often invite the fattest clergy to stay and then, after dinner, make them race round the house against each other. If he invited the clergy wives he always sprinkled flour outside their bedroom doors to see if he could catch them moving about between bedrooms during the night.

In his latter years he travelled extensively in France and Italy, and spent so lavishly that many hotels bear his name to this day; his cook always rode on ahead of his carriage so that his food would be ready when he arrived at the next inn. After a while he received a 'round robin' criticising him for being absent for so long from his parish, but he sent each signatory an inflated pig's bladder containing a dried pea along with a copy of the following verse:

> Three large bluebottles sat upon three bladders.
> Blow bottle flies, blow; burst, blow bladder burst
> A new-blown bladder and three blue balls
> Make a great rattle. So rattle bladder rattle.

He died in 1803 aged seventy-three.

A LIFE DEVOTED TO WATER

Lord Rokeby

Mathew Robinson, afterwards Lord Rokeby, was born in 1712 at Hythe in Kent and studied at Westminster and Trinity College, Cambridge. In later life he was mostly celebrated for the length of his beard and for his total addiction to bathing; by the time he came into his inheritance in 1754 – his father was a wealthy landowner and gentleman usher to George II – his beard had reached his knees. He drank neither tea, coffee nor alcohol, and always ate off a wooden plate. His most remarkable trait was that, having built a bathing hut at Hythe, he swam each day until so exhausted that he had to be dragged from the water.

Each day he could be seen heading slowly towards the beach, bent double, a wizened figure dressed entirely in black, walking ahead of his grandest carriage with a favourite servant walking behind in his finest livery. If it rained he would stay out in the rain and tell his servants to ride in the carriage because, unlike him, they were not used to the water: 'They are gaudily dressed,' he once explained to an acquaintance, 'and might therefore spoil their clothes and occasion an illness.'

Later in his life he gave up going to the beach and built a bath by his house. His neighbour, a Mr Kirby, reported seeing him one day: 'I saw him dart from his bathing house, entirely naked but with his beard tucked under one arm and followed by his dogs.'

Rokeby drank only beef tea and water, but was said by the locals to eat human flesh; probably this assumption arose from the time he was found in his bath with a large joint of veal floating by him from which, periodically, he took large bites. By the time he reached his eighties he was still bathing for hours each day. He built a public drinking fountain in the middle of the highway near his house and if he came across anyone partaking of the beverage he believed in above all others he would often reward them with a half-crown.

Just as he refused to cut or even trim his beard, so he refused to see any of the trees or hedges on his land interfered with in any way; they were all allowed to grow wild and untouched for decades. For years, too, he refused to allow any of his tenants to sow barley because, he argued, the barley would go to a maltster who paid taxes that were used to continue the war with France which he thought unjust.

Nearing the end of his life and fearing that a dreadful seizure was about to take hold of him, he told his nephew that he was 'welcome to stay, but if, out of a false humanity you should call in medical assistance and it should accidentally happen that I am not killed by the doctor, I hope I will have sufficient use of my hands and senses left to make a new will and disinherit you'. He died in 1800 aged eighty-eight.

THE WORLD'S MOST ABSENT-MINDED MAN

The Reverend George Harvest

Educated at Oxford, George Harvest first tried to become an actor. When that failed he took holy orders and decided to get married, but he was so forgetful that when the great day dawned he went fishing, not returning until nightfall. Only then did he remember that he should have been at the village church.

He was the parish priest of Thames Ditton in Surrey for more than thirty years, and in that time turned absentmindedness into an art form. However, despite his extraordinary forgetfulness he was a good-hearted man and much liked, and it was this as well as the forbearance of his flock that kept him in a job for so long.

Often when he wrote a letter he would write it to one person, address it to a second and post it to a third. Paying a visit to London he passed a beggar in the street, and when the beggar raised his hat in hopes of being given a penny, Harvest was in such a dream that he merely thought it was an acquaintance and raised his hat in return.

When he needed to travel he almost always had to borrow a horse, for he usually mislaid his own horses after a few days. But he had a terrible tendency to lose the borrowed ones too, and eventually no one would lend him a horse no matter how dire was the emergency.

Whenever he had dinner at a friend's house he would try to leave by going up instead of downstairs, and he invariably got lost on the way home. He often went into his neighbour's house at night thinking he was at home, and would then be found fast asleep in the wrong bed.

Towards the end of his life he made a second marriage proposal and was accepted. On the day of the wedding he woke early, and finding the weather wonderful he wandered off to Richmond, met some friends and passed a delightful day without so much as a glimmer of memory that his bride-to-be and her family would be waiting for him some miles off.

In Calais once he managed to get separated from his friends and, speaking no French but keen to get back to his hotel, the Silver Lion, he 'put a silver shilling in his mouth and set himself in the attitude of a lion rampant...and after exciting much admiration was led back to the inn by a soldier who thought he was a maniac escaped from his keepers'.

On another occasion in London he was sitting in a box watching a play when his old and very grubby nightcap fell off his head and into the theatre pit, where it was thrown backwards and forwards by the audience. Afraid it would never be returned to him, Harvest stood up in the middle of the play and preached for ten minutes, concluding that 'it is a very serious thing to die without a nightcap'. To which he added: 'I shall be restless tonight if I have not my cap'. Obviously the people were struck with his manner, because the cap was handed back up to him at the end of a stick.

Although he was a kind-hearted man, Dr Harvest frequently got into trouble. At a grand dinner with Lady Onslow and a number of distinguished guests he spotted a large fly on his neighbour's bonnet. He leapt to his feet and shouted 'May you be married!' at the top of his voice and struck the woman a violent blow on the head. In fact he hit her so hard he knocked her out.

George Harvest died in 1789 aged sixty-one.

THE CHEATING VICAR

Lord Frederick Beauclerk

Born in 1773, Beauclerk was the great-grandson of Charles II and Nell Gwyn. When he was in his twenties he became vicar of St Albans in Hertfordshire, but he had already developed the two passions that were to dominate his life: cricket and horse racing. Indeed he was so passionate about both sports that he cheated continually.

At cricket he bribed both the players and the scorers regularly – he claimed that in one year he earned £600 by rigging matches – and despite the fact that he was actually a very good player, whenever he played a match against a team whose members did not know him he couldn't resist pretending he was either injured or disabled. He would set off from the pavilion towards the wicket with an exaggerated limp, or with huge quantities of packing either up the back of his shirt or under one shoulder. If he was known by the opposing team he would deliberately provoke the bowlers by hanging his gold watch on the middle wicket, and then taunt them with their inability to hit it. In spite of his eccentricities he became president of the MCC in 1825 – only to quit a year later, furious that overarm bowling was to be allowed.

When he wasn't playing cricket he was invariably to be found at Kempton Park or Epsom, but he didn't just bet, he also rode – although fearing his bishop would discover what he was up to, he rode under a series of assumed names. Such was his love of the horse that he always preached from a saddle specially fitted into his pulpit. He died in 1850.

DINING WITH THE DOGS

Francis Henry Egerton, Earl of Bridgwater

A small man with a delicate constitution, Francis Henry Egerton was born in the early eighteenth century. As an adult he went everywhere accompanied by two huge lackeys who would walk one on each side of him, and to make sure that he went unnoticed he wore an enormous sugarloaf hat pulled well down over his eyes.

He was always extraordinarily polite, and if he borrowed a book from a friend he would insist on returning it in his finest carriage. It would be unaccompanied, however, so friends would hear a knock at the door and open it to discover a magnificent landau, four footmen in full livery – and their book.

A great lover of dogs, Egerton would sometimes go on foot while his carriage conveyed a dozen of his favourites. He worried terribly about the state of their feet – though they hardly ever walked anywhere – and paid the local shoemaker to make boots for them all; but then, Egerton had a thing about boots: he wore a new pair himself every day, and when he took them off at night he would line them up in perfect rows. No one else was ever allowed to touch them. He took great pleasure in judging how the year had passed by looking at their state of wear.

Every day his vast and magnificent dining-table was laid for a dozen guests, but no one was ever invited to the house and Egerton would always dine with twelve of his dogs. Each was provided with a napkin which would be fixed on its collar, and each had a servant standing behind ready to wait on it. Apparently the dogs had grown so used to all this that they behaved very well. If they did misbehave they were banished for a day or more to the kitchen and a diet of bread and water.

A COAT FOR ALL SEASONS

The Reverend Mr Jones

A high Victorian and notorious miser, Mr Jones wore the same hat and coat every day for almost fifty years and when, finally, his hat fell to pieces, he was spotted stealing one from a scarecrow! He was constantly mistaken for a beggar, which he enjoyed immensely. By the time he died his coat was so patched and repaired that the villagers decided to preserve it in a glass case in the village hall, where it remains to this day.

THE CARDBOARD CONGREGATION

Father Denham

Father Denham of Warleggan in Cornwall died in 1953, but for at least a decade before that no one had ever come to his regular Sunday services because when they did turn up he was incredibly rude to them. Unperturbed by this, Father Denham simply made cardboard parishioners which he propped up in the pews. Ramblers passing near the church on Sundays would hear him delivering an apparently passionate sermon to his cardboard flock. So antisocial did he become that, eventually, he fitted a high barbed-wire fence right round his house. Why he bothered is difficult to say because the house contained not a stick of furniture. It was believed in the villages round about that Father Denham lived entirely on nettles and porridge.

A CALENDAR OF BRITISH ECCENTRICITIES

There follows just a small selection of the many weird and wonderful events which take place at various times of the year throughout the country.

JANUARY

New Year's Day Boys' and Men's Ba, Kirkwall, Orkney

Two huge teams play ancient football. Each side consists of an unlimited number of men who try to take the ball (ba) to their own goal. The other 'team' tries to stop them, and the goalposts are at each end of the town. Also takes place on Christmas Day.

Hood Game, Haxey, Humberside

Held on 6 January (the pre-1752 calendar Christmas Day). An ancient game where huge crowds attempt to push the 'hood' (a thick rope bound in leather) into one of the 'goals' (pubs).

Burning of the Clavie, Burghead, Grampian

A large torch is burned on 11 January (pre-1752 New Year's Eve) to mark the end of the old year.

Charles I Commemoration

Five hundred members of the English Civil War Society dressed in seventeenth-century clothes lay a wreath at the site of Charles I's execution in London in 1649.

Maldon Mud Race, Maldon, Essex

The dirtiest, vilest charity event ever. Competitors race along the bed of the river Blackwater, which is normally feet-deep in thick black mud.

Up Helly Aa, Lerwick, Shetland Isles

After a torchlit procession a Viking longship is ceremonially burned to make the end of Yule.

FEBRUARY

Annual Grimaldi Service

Nearly 100 clowns gather in a church in East London to thank God for clowns.

Shrove Tuesday Skipping Festival, Scarborough, North Yorkshire

There are numerous skipping and pancake races, and the mayor of the town rings a pancake bell to start the event.

Shrove Tuesday Football Match, Ashbourne, Derbyshire
Held between the Up'ards and the Down'ards; an ancient game of football is played through the area, with the goals (mills) 3 miles apart. A football game – Jethart Ba' – also takes place in Jedburgh, Scotland.

MARCH
Spring Equinox Ceremony
Held each year near Tower Hill in London. The chief druid watches over processions, trumpet calls and the ceremony of the sheathing of the sword.

Whuppity Stourie (or Scourie), Lanark
Local children pursue each other around the church three times, beating each other with paper balls on strings.

Good Friday, Tinsley Green, West Sussex
Venue for the world marbles championships.

APRIL
Numerous Easter Egg hunts; notable ones at Crealy Park, Clyst St Mary in Devon and at Wakefield in Yorkshire.

Easter Frolics at Keighley, West Yorkshire
Jugglers, stiltwalkers and Easter bonnet parades throughout the town.

World Coal Carrying Championship, Osset, West Yorkshire
Ladies carry a 25kg bag of coal in a 1-mile race; men have to manage a 50kg sack.

Hocktide at Hungerford, Berkshire
The men of the town, known as tutti, visit the houses of the commoners during the second week after Easter to collect a penny per head. The tutti throw pennies to the children as they go along; Maypole dancing and clog dancing in the streets.

Amberley Veteran Cycle Day, Arundel, Sussex
Cycle race for ancient bikes: boneshakers from the 1870s-90s, penny farthings etc.

Sailors' Hobby Horse, Minehead, Somerset
Ancient ceremony on the eve of Mayday where a horse made in the shape of a boat is paraded through the streets surrounded by dancers.

MAY
Jack in the Green, Hastings, Sussex
More than 800 clog dancers, giants and mummers gather together.

Hobby Horse, Padstow, Cornwall
An ancient custom which starts on May Day eve; on May Day the Hobby Horse and the Club Man dance through the streets of the village.

Weymouth Kite Flying Festival, Dorset
The biggest in Britain; it attracts hundreds of fanatical kite flyers.

World Stilton Cheese Rolling Championship, Stilton, Peterborough
Held on the hill outside the village's two oldest pubs. Cheese rolling also takes place at Cooper's Hill, Brockworth, Gloucestershire.

Robert Dover's Cotswold Olympick Games, Dovers Hill, Gloucestershire
Traditional games and competitions, which started in 1612. The day ends with a bonfire, and a procession into Chipping Camden.

Penny Hedge Planting, Whitby, Yorkshire
The hedge has been planted on Ascension Eve since the twelfth century; it has to be planted on the shore below high-water mark, and has to stand for three tides.

Man v Horse Marathon, Llanwrtyd Wells, Powys
A 22-mile race through the mountains, pitting teams of men and horses against each other.

JUNE
Ythan Raft Race, Ellon, Aberdeenshire
The biggest raft race in the UK.

Annual Scottish Canal Jumping Championships, Ratho, Edinburgh
Hundreds of competitors try to leap the 36ft wide canal using an 18ft pole.

JULY
World Championship Pea Shooting, Witcham, nr Ely, Cambridgeshire
Target and distance shooting to find the World Champion.

International Brick and Rolling-pin Championships, Stroud, Gloucestershire
A competition between the four villages bearing the name of Stroud (worldwide), held on the same day and at the same time in each country. Women throw the rolling-pins, and men throw the bricks, in teams of six.

AUGUST
The Burryman, South Queensferry, Lothian
On the day before the Ferry Fair, a silent man, dressed as a living 'bush', walks for 7 miles through the town, receiving gifts.

Reptile Revels, Ormskirk, Lancashire
A celebration of all things reptilian.

Sedan Chair Race, Tunbridge Wells, Kent
Competitors must carry their passenger, stop for cake, apple bobbing and to take the spring waters.

World Bog Snorkelling Championships, Llanwrtyd Wells, Powys
Competitors swim underwater along a muddy, weed-filled ditch.

SEPTEMBER
Horn Dance, Abbots Bromley, Hertfordshire
Six dancers dress up in antler horns and dance before the villagers.

British Town Criers Championship, Hastings, Sussex

OCTOBER
World Conker Championships, Ashton, nr Peterborough

Taunton Cider Barrel Race
Twelve two-person teams have to push a 9 gallon barrel uphill for a mile.

NOVEMBER
Burning Tar Barrels, Ottery St Mary, Devon
Tar barrels are lit and then rolled and carried through the crowded streets.

DECEMBER
Mummers Play, Moulton, Northampton
Held on Boxing Day.

Biggar Ne'erday Bonfire, Lanarkshire
A druid bonfire to encourage the sun to rise back into the sky and bring back the longer days of spring and summer.

Stonehaven Fireball Ceremony, Grampian, Scotland
The swinging of fireballs is an ancient year's end ceremony, intended to ward off evil spirits.

Acknowledgements

Tales of the Country Eccentrics owes its existence to the marvellous characters who agreed to be interviewed, and to: Sue Hall of David & Charles, Alex Webb-Peploe, John Paley, John Williams Taylor of the Museum of Rural Life in Wales, Rhian Taylor, John Humphreys, Colin Willock, Fred J. Taylor, Brian Martin, Nicola Bird, Phil Drabble, Tony Jackson, Sally Brown, Kevin Pilley, Lol Plummer, Deborah Fisher, Barbara Thompson, Louise Clark, Karen Warren, Colin Jackson, Sarah Storey, Jane Simms, Mary Corbett, Corinna Button, Megan Rule, Anne Soward, Andrea Spain and Cheryl Barnard.

Index